DROPKICK

MURPHY

DROP
KICK

HAMILCAR
PUBLICATIONS
BOSTON

KICK
PHY

A LEGENDARY LIFE

EMILY SWEENEY

FORWARD BY
KEN CASEY
OF THE DROPKICK MURPHYS

ISBN: 978-1-949590-64-7

CIP data is available.

hamilcarpubs.com

Aut viam inveniam aut faciam

*For Dr. John "Dropkick" Murphy and his family,
especially his children: Richard, David, John,
Michael, Marie, Susan, and Amy*

CONTENTS

FOREWORD

I was lucky enough to get into recovery at a young age, and I would hear a lot of older gentlemen—who were instrumental in helping me turn my life around—talk about the time they had spent at Dropkick Murphy's Bellows Farm, and their experiences there. I had also heard my grandfather and some other family members talk about it.

And there was a point in my life when I felt like I could not get away from the term "Dropkick Murphy's." At the same time, I was forming a band—one that we weren't taking very seriously. We started the band to win a thirty-dollar bet that I made with a coworker. The bet was that I couldn't form a band on three weeks' notice to open for my friend's band, so we had three weeks to come up with the band name. And the name Dropkick Murphy was just everywhere I went, so we used that as our band name. We liked that it paid tribute to a local legend.

When we started to gain some popularity, playing all-ages shows at the Rat, we would silk-screen our own T-shirts and sell them for five bucks, so we would sell a lot of them at that bargain price. Inevitably, the next show all these young kids would be coming back, saying "Hey, what the hell is this place? I have old guys stopping me all over the place, telling me, 'I was there in 1965 or whenever. . . .'" It was in those early days—before the band really became known and recognizable—that we would often get fans who were perplexed as to why old guys with red noses were stopping them to tell them stories about Bellows Farm.

Ninety percent of the stuff I knew about Dropkick's came from the mouths of old timers who were there, but you gotta remember: they were in a fog. A lot of their stories didn't necessarily add up, because they weren't exactly in the best frame of mind when they were arriving there. So it's nice to have the facts documented in this book and proper tribute be paid to the man, the myth, the legend—John "Dropkick" Murphy.

Ken Casey
Boston
December 2022

INTRODUCTION

The Dropkick Murphys have toured the world, sold millions of records, and their music is played in sports stadiums across the country. If you've ever heard "I'm Shipping Up to Boston," the song that was featured in Martin Scorsese's 2006 Oscar-winning film *The Departed*, then you're familiar with their work. But although the Dropkick Murphys have achieved rock-star status and grown into a global phenomenon, not everyone knows the true story behind the band's name and the incredible man who inspired them.

This book, for the first time ever, chronicles the remarkable life of Dr. John "Dropkick" Murphy, a professional wrestler who put himself through osteopathic medical school during the Great Depression and then went on to open Bellows Farm, a beloved institution that was both a facility where top-of-the-line athletes could train and a secluded place where down-on-their-luck alcoholics could go to sober up discreetly.

Dropkick Murphy spent the better part of three decades helping people who were battling alcoholism. But after he closed his detox center, people's memories faded, and Dropkick's once-famous sanitarium became a piece of forgotten history. Dropkick's farm was occasionally mentioned in books and articles, but eventually its very location and purpose became obscured by the passage of time. I read one book that claimed Dropkick Murphy's farm was in Athol; then I found another book that said it was in Fitchburg. Yet another book described it as a secret hangout where Catholic priests and politically connected men could go and get drunk in private.

Even Ken Casey, the bassist and co-founder of the Dropkick Murphys, didn't know the exact location of Dropkick Murphy's farm for many years. But he listened to many stories about it.

"I was just always curious about the place, and I'd heard a lot about it, but it was almost like this fictional, mythical place," said Casey.

Casey said men who went to Dropkick's told all kinds of tales about the farm and what went on there.

"It was interesting, it was kind of almost like a folklore, because the state of mind of guys who were going up there, going up there to clean up, maybe their memory wasn't the clearest, you know?" said Casey. "You'd hear all these varying descriptions of it."

As a result, an air of mystique surrounded Dropkick Murphy's farm. But I didn't give this much thought until one evening several years ago, when I was sitting in Crossroads, one of my favorite restaurants in Acton, Massachusetts.

Crossroads is an old-fashioned pub with a long mahogany bar that draws a loyal following of regular customers who sit in the same seats every day. On this particular evening, I overheard someone mention Dropkick Murphy, and my ears perked up. At first, I thought they were talking about the band from Boston. No, they said. They were talking about the *real* Dropkick Murphy, the man for whom the band was named. Once upon a time, they told me, Dropkick Murphy lived nearby, on a vast farm in Acton, where he ran a sanitarium for alcoholics and hosted famous guests.

"How far away?" I asked.

"Just down the street," they said.

From that point on, I was intrigued. I wanted to learn more about this mysterious place and the man who started it. What I discovered both surprised me and inspired me.

Why does this story still matter? While I was writing this book, I had the opportunity to speak with Linda McMahon, the former CEO of the WWE, and we talked about how Dropkick Murphy's story is still so relevant today.

McMahon knows professional wrestling well. Her husband, Vince McMahon, is a third-generation wrestler promoter, and together they built the WWE into the largest professional wrestling company in the world.

We discussed how Dropkick Murphy launched his career in the middle of the Great Depression, and how her husband's grandfather, Jess McMahon, worked in the business back then and saw firsthand how people would continue to attend wrestling shows, even when they didn't have much money to spare.

"It's definitely a form of escape," she said. "I think in tough times, we all look for forms of escape."

And the theatrical side of pro wrestling sets it apart from other sports. That held true in Dropkick Murphy's day, and it still holds true today.

"It's a soap opera," said McMahon. "If wrestling were just matches in the ring, as athletic and wonderful as they might be to watch, they wouldn't be nearly as meaningful if they weren't telling a story."

McMahon marvels at how much creativity goes into developing the characters in pro wrestling. The storylines behind each wrestler's motivations and reasons for being in the ring are constantly evolving. There are professional rivalries. Sibling jealousies. Long-running feuds. Title challenges. Double-crosses. Injuries and medical issues. Those are just some examples of the undercurrents that propel the stories forward, making fans want to come back for more.

"There have always been themes and plots and subplots, which make it so entertaining," she said.

Another aspect of wrestling that hasn't changed is the amount of training and preparation that's involved. McMahon believes pro wrestlers are among the most well-conditioned athletes and performers in the world. And in some respects, they have to be: Unlike many other sports, there is no offseason.

Professional wrestlers have to develop not only strength, but also mobility and stamina. McMahon noted that the most successful wrestlers are all about self-improvement. Dropkick Murphy was no different.

Dropkick Murphy "was so very much interested in being in good physical condition, but also eating right and just really taking care of his physical well-being," she said.

And, in many ways, he was ahead of his time.

1

ALL SAINTS' EVE

*"The art of living is more like wrestling than dancing,
insofar as it stands ready against the accidental and
the unforeseen, and is not apt to fall."*
—Roman Emperor Marcus Aurelius

There's nothing like the feeling of getting dropkicked in the face.

WHAP!

The first boot hits you. You see it coming. Your eyelids instinctively shut tight. A booming thud reverberates through your skull when a dusty sole, concealing one very heavy human foot, strikes your head. You feel the powerful thump as the boot collides with your chin. Your jaw slams shut. Your teeth clash together. A second boot hits your neck and your head jerks back. Your brow furrows. A burst of white light flashes before your eyes. The skin on your forehead creases and folds, absorbing the impact. Jowls whiplash. Cheeks jiggle. Then you fall to the mat and lay there for a moment, with your face pressed against the grimy canvas. Gasping to catch your breath, your chest heaves up and down. You slowly open your eyes, straining to regain focus and balance. You can hear voices of people screaming your name from a few feet away. They're heckling you.

"How do you like that?"

"C'mon . . . fight 'im!"

"Give it to him!"

"Kill 'im!"

You lift your head from the canvas and glance upward. You see a pair of dark leather wrestling boots, with white cotton laces, gently bouncing, from one foot to the other, from one foot to the other. Those shoes belong to Dropkick Murphy, and he's ready to pounce on you again.

It was that sensational spectacle that John "Dropkick" Murphy skill-fully delivered to his opponents and fans, time and time again, week after week, in wrestling rings all over the country. The dropkick was his specialty, his signature move, one that he practiced regularly and would become famous for.

Dropkick Murphy may have pondered this as he left his home in Medford and traveled into Boston for his next wrestling match.

On Tuesday, October 31, 1933, Murphy was twenty-one years old. Athletic and able, he was a blond-haired, blue-eyed, fresh-faced rookie still new to the world of professional wrestling.

That evening he was scheduled to wrestle at the Mechanics Hall, a magnificent Victorian fortress that stood like a sentry on Huntington Avenue. With brick walls over two feet thick, it was a colossal bully of a building that occupied its own street corner, on a triangular patch of land next to the Boston & Albany railroad yards in the Back Bay section of Boston, not far from Copley Square.

Constructed by the Massachusetts Charitable Mechanics Association in 1881, it stood proudly as a grand temple honoring blue-collar work-ers and an elegant monument to craftsmanship. The landmark building had been built by tradesmen, for tradesmen, at a time when many people didn't have life-insurance policies, and social clubs and similar organiza-tions provided a safety net for workers and their families.

The Mechanics Building was one of the biggest auditoriums in the city. It was used as a convention center and venue for concerts, political rallies, track meets, boxing matches, and exhibitions of every sort—candy shows, dog shows, poultry shows, flower shows, boat shows, car shows. Tonight, it was a wrestling show.

And for Murphy, this was the big time.

Murphy was just starting out in the business of professional wrestling, and he wanted to make a name for himself. Wrestling promoter Charlie Gordon had expressed interest in him because of his athletic ability and his looks—Murphy's prominent cheekbones, square jaw, gentle eyes, flaxen hair, and muscular physique made him a perfect candidate for the mat game. His Irish surname bolstered his box-office appeal in Boston, a city so Irish that it was nicknamed the "Dublin of America." One in five Bostonians was originally from the Emerald Isle or had at least one parent who'd been born there. There were thousands of Murphys listed in the city directory, and having an Irishman on the wrestling card helped fill seats.

Charlie Gordon staged weekly shows at the Mechanics Building on Tuesday nights. The forty-four-year-old promoter was always on the lookout for new talent. He specialized in middleweights and light heavyweights, so most of his fighters weighed less than 190 pounds. In his view, they were the perfect size: "not too big to be slow, and large enough to be strong," he'd say. Gordon saw potential in Murphy and asked him to play the role of a clean-cut wrestler, a good guy who followed the rules. If the audience responded to his performance in the ring, there was a chance he could become a headliner someday.

As he made his way to the wrestling match, Murphy would have seen Boston's urban skyline. Chimneys and smokestacks stood out on the horizon of the city like dark skinny matchsticks spewing out puffy clouds of smoke, steam, and soot.

A lonely skyscraper known as the Custom House Tower loomed large above the smaller buildings in downtown Boston. Its ornate Italian Renaissance steeple pierced the clear sky, making it stand out as the tallest point in the city. The soaring clock tower was more than twice the height of the factories, hotels, tenements, warehouses, and businesses that surrounded it. To young people who lived outside the city, it was a beacon of hope and opportunity, and for Murphy, potential fame and fortune.

Murphy may have thought about what people in Boston would be doing in the next several hours, and perhaps wondered how many of them would actually show up to watch him wrestle on this Halloween night.

The whole month of October had been chilly. But the 31st turned out to be unseasonably warm. The temperature reached 67 degrees in the afternoon and hovered around 60 degrees when night fell. It felt like springtime.

There was a jovial feeling in the air that evening, a sense of elation mixed with cautious hope, combined with apprehension of the unknown.

On that particular Halloween in Boston, hard liquor could be had quite easily—but not legally. Prohibition was still in effect, although the days of the Volstead Act were numbered. Twenty-nine states had already voted in favor of repealing it. Everyone sensed that Prohibition would be coming to an end soon.

The city of Boston was still reveling in the relatively new phenomenon of 3.2 percent beer, which had become legal in April. Bay Staters flocked to restaurants, hotel bars, food markets, and drug stores to drink it. Ten million gallons of the new legal brew had been sold in just six months. "Beer on Tap" signs were everywhere.

Out on the darkening streets of Boston, children dressed as witches, goblins, ghosts, cowboys, and Indians skipped and scampered through the streets. Several girls wore flapper dresses and red lipstick, with their eyebrows shaped into pencil-thin arches so they could sashay down the sidewalk looking like their favorite wise-cracking movie star, Mae West.

The odor of burnt leaves hung over certain parts of the city as costumed mischief-makers struck matches to light bonfires on darkened streets. The air was filled with laughter and singing, and the occasional sound of glass shattering, as boys threw rocks at streetlamps.

Other pranksters cut clotheslines down and used white chalk to scribble across the windows and windshields of automobiles. They also pulled fire alarms—lots of them. Gongs went off at fire stations all over the city, one after another, and firefighters grew increasingly frustrated as they responded to a continuous stream of unnecessary calls as the night of merrymaking wore on.

Out on the streets, there was a cacophony of bells ringing, horns blaring, noisemakers clacking and rattling. The city was alive.

Adults of all ages flocked to hotels and nightclubs and speakeasies. Dance halls were festooned with orange and black crepe paper, and images of witches and black cats.

That evening, girls at Simmons College were hosting a hobo party. Students cut holes and sewed patches on their clothes in an effort to create the perfect vagabond outfit, with a prize awarded for the best costume.

The Raymor Ballroom, a low-slung, art deco dance hall at 253 Huntington Avenue, was hosting a Halloween celebration with Jack Brown and his Bal-a-l'air Orchestra. It was billed as his first Boston appearance. Admission was forty cents, and attendees were promised noisemakers, party favors, and souvenirs to take home.

Over on Piedmont Street, couples were streaming into the Cocoanut Grove nightclub for a special dinner followed by a huge Halloween celebration with floor shows and dancing to the music of Ranny Weeks and his orchestra.

Upstairs at Cascades, the rooftop nightclub atop the Hotel Bradford, the festivities were starting early. Lew Conrad's orchestra was playing lively tunes for the men and women who'd gathered on the dance floor, fourteen floors above the city. Later that night, live entertainment would be provided by Lou Walters' Revue—a troupe of twenty dancing starlets who promised to provide audiences with "over one hour of speed, beauty, and rhythm."

Over at the Palais Royal at 281 Huntington Avenue, there would be dancing until 3 a.m., and no cover charge. The club promised it would be "Boston's Greatest Halloween" with plenty of "mirth, glamorous girls, and alluring dancers." Music would be provided by Jimmy Gallagher and his Melody Boys.

At the Old Howard, the infamous burlesque house in bustling Scollay Square, the "Prosperity Girls" dance troupe would be entertaining male patrons with chorus-line kicks and scanty outfits.

Moviegoers were lining up at theaters to see the hip-wiggling Mae West and her younger leading man, Cary Grant, in *I'm No Angel*. At the Strand Theater in Malden, they were watching *Gold Diggers of 1933*, a film about a super-wealthy composer who puts unemployed Broadway actors to work in a new play. The movie opened with a lively musical number, featuring dozens of showgirls wearing high heels and bikinis made of shimmering coins. The girls smiled coyly and danced, hoisting oversized coins above their heads and kicking their bare legs in the air, while a wide-eyed Ginger Rogers stared at the screen, blinking her long lashes, singing the song that became one of the biggest hits of the year, an auditory antidote to the symptoms of the Great Depression:

We're in the money, we're in the money;
We've got a lot of what it takes to get along!
We're in the money, that sky is sunny,
Old Man Depression you are through, you done us wrong.

A movie ticket cost about the same as a wrestling ticket. Would people pay the same price to see Dropkick Murphy as they would to see a line of chorus girls singing and dancing on the silver screen?

Murphy certainly hoped so.

If he was concerned about how many people would show up, he was right to be. The Depression wasn't over yet—not even close—and people were being careful with their money. In the city of Boston alone, 98,000 people were out of work. In some neighborhoods, the unemployment rate had reached 40 percent.

To get to the Mechanics Building, Murphy had to walk along Huntington Avenue, a broad boulevard lined with brownstone apartment buildings. Two sets of streetcar tracks ran down the middle of the road. Trolleys rumbled past, with bells clanging, their metal wheels squealing as they rolled along the steel rails, pulling cars filled with people en route to masquerade parties and other Halloween celebrations.

After the sun went down, cast iron streetlamps glowed, illuminating the sidewalk on Huntington Avenue. Rays of moonlight shone down and reflected off the chrome, winged hood ornaments of Chevrolets and Plymouths, traced the graceful curves of the steel fenders on Ford Model A and B sedans, and gleamed off of the boxy roofs of Essex coupes parked along the brick and concrete sidewalks.

Murphy looked ahead as he made his way toward the imposing temple of red brick before him.

The Mechanics Building was a familiar landmark, a grand superstructure with an octagonal tower and gigantic turret that stretched 90 feet up toward the sky. Its strong red-brick facade was adorned with terra-cotta ornamentation and caps and sills made of freestone. The massive building ran the length of two football fields along Huntington Avenue.

Murphy eventually reached the stone masonry steps that led to the entrance of the Mechanics Building. When he went inside the grand hall, he would have seen that its roof soared more than two-and-a-half stories upward to a clerestory made of metal and glass. The cathedral-like structure was supported by graceful dark wooden trusses that swooped across the ceiling. The lower balcony was adorned with elegant wooden trefoil molding.

Inside that vast space, a musty smell hung in the air, a mix of stale cigar smoke and salty popcorn and roasted peanuts. It was still early, and all of the seats in the cavernous Victorian auditorium were empty.

That night, Murphy would be facing off against Fred "The Bruiser" Bruno, a tough-looking, brutish grappler from New York who was known as the "Italian Roughneck."

Bruno was a rugged performer and a regular on the local wrestling circuit. His hair was dark and wavy, and he combed it to the sides, parting
it precisely in the middle. The part in his hair lined up perfectly with the
crease in the center of his forehead, which formed a dark line between his
intense dark eyes. His ears stuck out a bit, just like his bulbous nose and
the triangular patch of dark hair on his chest. When he was working in
the ring and playing the role of a bad guy, he wore a fierce scowl and his
lips turned down sternly.

His ears were swollen and stiff and permanently deformed from hitting
the mat so many times. The condition, known as "cauliflower ear," was
very common among wrestlers.

Bruno was about fifteen years older than Murphy, and the veteran of
the locker room.

Bruno and Murphy were one of the preliminary matches. Also on the
card that night were:

Winn Robbins vs. Dynamite Jones
Jack "Chocolate" Gans vs. Jose Firpo
Gardner Hindon vs. Dr. Altshuler
Mike Tellegen vs. George Dusette
Tony Papalino vs. The Blue Eagle

And the two main events were:

Jackie Nichols of New York vs. Ed Flowers of Cuba
The Great Mephisto of Germany vs. Ted Germaine of South Boston

Murphy most likely shared a dressing room with many of these wrestlers. Unlike other sports, in which opponents get ready in separate areas,
pro wrestlers usually dressed and undressed together in a common locker
room. Wrestling dressing rooms were interesting places, where big, burly
performers would go over the details of their matches while waiting to
enter the ring. Many played cards to pass the time while they waited for
their turn in the ring. It wasn't uncommon to see wrestlers sitting around
a table, holding tiny aces, kings, and queens in their large hands and playing a friendly game of poker, bantering about promoters and managers
and the latest rumors and gossip from the wrestling circuit. If they weren't

trading war stories from the mat, they'd often share tips on where to find the best cheap restaurants that served the most generous portions. Food was always a popular topic of discussion among wrestlers—they had to consume a lot of it, every single day, to maintain their muscular physiques.

Outside, the moon loomed large in the dark sky, casting a pale glow over the city of Boston.

Wrestling fans arrived in droves, stepping off trains and trolleys and hopping out of taxis. One by one, they streamed into the Mechanics Building and up to the ticket counters, where they plunked down Indian Head nickels and quarters—and the occasional crinkled bill—to pay the admission price. Some may have flashed discount cards and complimentary passes that Charlie Gordon had distributed leading up to the bout. Wrestling was a tough business, and Gordon had to hustle hard to fill the room every week. His discount passes drummed up publicity and allowed fans to get a balcony seat for free or buy a ringside seat for forty cents.

Inside the grand hall, excitement was building. It was electric. Anticipation spread throughout the room as the crowd assembled.

Charlie Gordon had blue eyes, a full head of neatly combed hair, and a strong nose and jaw. He wore suits, smoked cigars, and was rather quiet and kept to himself.

Before each wrestling show, another man named Harry "Whitey" Kaunfer often stood watch outside of the main entrance to the Mechanics Building. Whitey was anything but quiet.

As Gordon's ringside announcer, Kaunfer had a booming voice. He usually stationed himself on the stone steps before matches, greeting fans like a politician, welcoming them with a hearty "Hello!"

Whitey got his nickname from his platinum-blond hair. His eyebrows and eyelashes were so fair, they looked almost white. But his voice was his calling card. He was a short man, but what he lacked in stature he made up for with his vocal cords. ("You're either born an announcer, or you aren't," he once said. "I just got natural volume. I just open up and let it out.") The *Boston Globe* nicknamed him "Boston's loudest citizen" and "Leatherlungs"; he was a spark plug of energy, with rosy cheeks and a huge smile.

Whitey always dressed well for sporting events: white collared shirt, a tightly knotted tie, pinstriped pants, vest, and jacket, with a handkerchief neatly tucked into the front pocket of his suit.

Standing guard at the entrance, Whitey's eyes would dart around quickly, counting heads as they walked past. How many people would show up that night? That number was not only important to him, but even more so to Gordon.

"Hello!" Whitey would say, flashing his white teeth with a big smile. Unknowing fans who didn't immediately recognize him would usually stop and turn their heads when they heard his familiar gruff voice.

Once he had an idea of the attendance, Whitey would grab the sleeve of an usher, lean in, and whisper (as best he could manage) into his ear: "Tell Charlie it looks like thirty-five." The usher would nod. That meant attendance could reach up to 3,500 that night.

During most weekday wrestling matches at the Mechanics Building, there were plenty of empty seats for the taking. On that Halloween night, rays of moonlight poured through the clerestory windows above the main auditorium, reflecting off the grand trusses that stretched across the auditorium ceiling and roof. Down below, in the center of it all, was the roped ring. Men walked up the steps, with their ticket stubs in their hands, searching for their seats.

Finally, it was time.

Murphy strode out of the dressing room and made his way to the ring. He walked down the darkened corridor until he emerged inside the auditorium.

Meanwhile, his opponent, Bruno, strutted down another aisle on the opposite side of the ring. Murphy pulled apart the top two ropes and stepped through them onto the canvas.

When the clock struck 8:30 p.m., it was showtime.

A loud voice from overhead suddenly crackled, and a thunderous voice boomed over the loudspeakers.

"Hello! Hello! Hello!"

Whitey Kaunfer always said these three words at the start of wrestling matches. It was his standard opening line, and it got the attention of the audience, who would yell back at him, in unison: "Hello, hello, hello!"

Up in the balcony, the chattering and chirping ceased, and conversations hushed to a murmur.

Whitey took a deep breath and began speaking into the microphone, reading the rules of the match. *"Preliminary bout! One fall to win, with a 15-minute time limit . . ."*

Whitey was thirty-three years old. He was born in Russia but grew up in Boston's West End, so he spoke with a thick Boston accent, and his gravelly delivery made him sound much older. His powerful voice resonated through the hall.

"from Medfooooord, Massachusetts, weighing 175 pounds, Johnneeeeey "Drrrr—opkickkkkk" Murphyyyyy!

Whitey would then pause for a moment and look down at the paper before him.

"And from New YUCK, weighing 176 pounds, Frrrrred Brunoooo!"

Like most out-of-state challengers, Bruno's introduction was likely met with sparse applause, as well as a few jeers, hisses, and boos.

Whitey would then take his hat and place it over the microphone.

Almost all wrestling matches started off with the same ritual. The referee, who typically wore a crisp, white short-sleeved shirt and pleated pants, would stand in the center of the ring, and both wrestlers would step out and approach him. They stood a few feet apart, snarling and staring each other down. The referee might then proceed to check their legs to make sure they weren't covered with grease or oil (which would make it easy to slip out of holds) and that they weren't hiding any foreign objects in their boots or trunks. He would also inspect their fingernails, to make sure they were trimmed short enough to prevent them from scratching each other's skin. Then the referee would recite instructions and the rules for their match: No choking. No hair pulling. No elbows. No knees.

The two contestants would nod, shake hands, and retreat to their respective corners, where they'd take off their robes.

DING!

After the timekeeper rang the bell, the crowd's murmurs escalated to shouts. Bruno and Murphy returned to the center of the mat, sizing each other up under the warm, pale glow of the lamps overhead, circling each other in the ring like lions stalking prey. Their eyes were locked on each other. Murphy held a defensive pose, with his knees bent, feet spread apart, body low, ready to attack.

They grunted and shuffled around the ring, scrambling to overpower each other. At one point during the scuffle, Murphy crouched down, and the tension in his upper thighs mounted, building up like a coiled spring, until the precise moment—just like he practiced and envisioned—that he pulled the trigger.

Murphy launched his muscular frame up, up, up into the air, a missile aimed at his target. The audience got quiet as his feet soared toward his opponent's head. Fans stood up from their seats and watched in amazement as Murphy, whose dropkick unfolded like a slow-motion film, toppled his opponent.

When Dropkick Murphy leaped into the air, time decelerated. The crowd left their seats, with their eyes widening, jaws open, cupping their hands around their lips, hollering, feeling a collective rush from what they were witnessing.

It was for brief split-seconds like these, thin slices of time, that the wrestlers and their audience were truly able to forget the concerns of their day-to-day lives. No longer were they mortals. Here, while watching a few rounds of wrestling, they were able to put aside their worries about the rent being late, crying babies, hungry children, angry bosses, sobbing wives, and low paychecks.

Professional wrestling was the perfect distraction for an uncertain time, considering the grim reality that most Americans faced as the country struggled to free itself from the stranglehold of the Great Depression. People were on edge and still getting used to feeling the unwelcome adrenalin rush and emotional pain that comes with not knowing where you'll get your next meal, how you'll pay your bills, or whether you'll find work the next day.

In the Mechanics Building that night, there was a sense of camaraderie. Every person in the room was there for the same thing: to enjoy the common experience that you get when you watch a movie in a sold-out theater, or a football game in a packed, roaring stadium. You're here, congregating in a sports temple, all of you, for the same reason. For those moments, taking place over a couple of hours of your life, the person sitting next to you is no longer a stranger. He's your newest neighbor, your friend, and you are bonded together.

Bruno and Murphy continued to tussle. Whitey looked at the time, then took his hat off the microphone. "Fiiiiiive minutes!" he called, hanging his hat on the microphone and sitting back.

The match continued until their time was up. Murphy's battle with Bruno ended in a draw. They had wrestled for fifteen minutes.

Murphy was still just a preliminary attraction, wrestling in one of several bouts that evening. There were many more to come. The night was far from over.

The first main event pitted "Tiger" Ed Flowers against Jackie Nichols. On the card Nichols was listed as a New Yorker, but he actually hailed from Presque Isle, Maine, and his real name was Samuel W. Nichols. Nichols was something of a veteran on the wrestling circuit. He'd been living on his own since he was a teenager and started wrestling in the 1920s.

That evening at the Mechanics Building, Nichols and Flowers wrestled for nearly thirty-three minutes straight until Nichols threw Flowers on his back and won the first fall. Flowers came back to win the second fall by applying a body press. Flowers then went on the attack and hurled himself at Nichols. But after enduring a series of these flying tackles, Nichols proved to be too quick for him, and suddenly stepped out of the way. Flowers barreled past him and got so tangled in the ropes that he reportedly dislocated his right leg. He couldn't return to the ring, and Nichols claimed victory by default.

The last bout of the evening featured the "Great Mephisto." His real name was Julius Woronick, and he was a young, hot-tempered wrestler from Meriden, Connecticut. He was a talented wrestler but also an alcoholic with a violent streak, especially toward his mother. Just a couple of years before, in January 1931, he had been arrested for assaulting his mother, which, sadly, was not an isolated incident.

Mephisto stood about five feet ten—the same height as Dropkick Murphy—and was marketed on the wrestling circuit as an inscrutable villain from Germany. He was featured on posters that billed him as a "Satanic Majesty" and "Mystery Man of the Mat" whose trademark move was a deadly piledriver.

"From Hamburg, Germany, in red tights, The Great Mephisto!"

Mephisto had a hunched-over stance. He stuck his neck out and stooped forward, with his neck hanging low so it aligned with his shoulders. He was quick and graceful and light on his feet and knew an array of moves and holds. He wore long, red-woolen tights and a tank top—from afar, it looked like he was wearing a singlet. He had dark, piercing eyes and black hair that he parted in the middle. It was shiny and greasy and looked to be slicked back by a dollop of pomade. His eyes were heavy lidded, and his high cheekbones, arching eyebrows, and plump lips made him look like a younger, more athletic version of Bela Lugosi in the role of Count Dracula.

"From South Boston, Ted Germaine!"

Ted Germaine had plenty of attitude. He had immigrated to the United States from Latvia as a child and still lived with his parents in an apartment on O Street in South Boston. He had spent the last few years on the wrestling circuit building his reputation as a heel who pulled all sorts of dirty tricks in the ring. Charlie Gordon described him as a "master at arousing hate" because his antics usually whipped the crowd into a frenzy. Germaine was known for biting his opponents and fighting with referees. He once unscrewed a glass lightbulb and used it as a weapon in a match.

Murphy may have stayed to watch the rest of the bouts. If he did, he would have wanted to study how Mephisto and Germaine operated in the ring. There was plenty of action to be seen.

Germaine bolted his eyes on his opponent.

The match was the best two falls out of three, and they went at it for a while. Nineteen minutes into the match, Mephisto grabbed Germaine's wrist, then quickly turned and flipped Germaine up and over his shoulder. Germaine's back hit the canvas with a booming thump that echoed through the auditorium. Mephisto had scored the first fall.

Germaine fought back hard. He kicked Mephisto, and then started pulling his hair and gouging his eyes. At that point the referee stepped in and warned Germaine to stop the foul play. Germaine turned his anger on the ref. It was at that moment that Mephisto saw his opportunity. Mephisto clenched his right fist and swung it up toward Germaine's head, punching him in the chin. Hard.

Germaine's head snapped back and swiveled as he absorbed the force of Mephisto's powerful uppercut. His lean body went limp as he slumped down to the mat. He laid there motionless in a crumpled, muscled heap, for five full minutes.

Mephisto was declared the winner. The crowd roared.

When all of the bouts were over, Murphy retreated to the dressing room, pulling off his wrestling boots and trunks, washing up before he headed home. The lights dimmed as the crowd exited the Mechanics Building. Wrestling fans buttoned their coats and braced themselves for the cool fall air as they filed out of the old exhibition hall and walked down the cold stone steps of the Mechanics Building.

It was then that Whitey would walk over to a telephone to complete one of his last tasks of the evening—reporting the results of the bouts to the local newspapers. Whitey knew the news business well. He put his booming voice to work early in his life, as a newsboy hawking papers on street corners, shouting "Pie-puhs! Pie-puhs!" to passersby. Now, as an adult, when he wasn't announcing sporting events, he drove a circulation truck for the *Boston Traveler*.

He would plug his finger into the rotary dial, turning one number at a time. The rotary dial *click-click-click-clicked* its way back to the starting position, and he continued dialing. Putting the phone to his mouth and ear, he would ask to talk to a journalist in the sports department and would rattle off the results of the matches that evening, If the editor had extra space to fill, he'd provide a play-by-play of what happened in the ring.

He would do the same for the Boston *Daily Record*, the *Boston Evening Transcript*, and the *Boston Post*. He wanted to make sure all of the next day's papers had the results of Charlie Gordon's show. Articles in the newspaper helped build publicity for Gordon's next event at the Mechanics Building, which was only a week away.

2

HOMETOWN BOY

"Medford rum! Ah, a breath of the Promised Land!"
—from the film *The Devil and Daniel Webster*

On Tuesday, December 12, 1933, Dropkick Murphy returned to the Mechanics Building for another match. He made his way to the auditorium that evening in subfreezing temperatures, as the Greater Boston area had been stuck in an icy spell for days,

Once again, Murphy hoped a decent-sized crowd would show up at the Mechanics Building. Not only was it cold, which might deter people from venturing outdoors, but Murphy and his colleagues now competed against the allure of bars and nightclubs that served alcohol. A week before, Prohibition had finally ended. Businessmen had scrambled to secure liquor licenses, and now licensed establishments across the city were pouring not only beer but cocktails of all kinds.

If Murphy was worried about how many people would turn out to watch wrestling on a Tuesday night in December, he now had more cause for concern. The familiar sound of ice dropping into glasses—clink, clink, clink—and the sizzling hiss of fizzy, bubbly, and breathtakingly intoxicating beverages filled everyone's cups and souls once again.

At bars all over the city, martinis and Bronx cocktails could be purchased legally for a quarter. Manhattans, bamboos, orange blossoms, and gin sours cost thirty cents. Clover clubs, rum cocktails, dubonnets, old-fashioneds, zazas, presidentes, rum rickeys, blended rye highballs, and rum highballs cost thirty-five cents.

Dropkick Murphy's opponent that night was Cliff Olson, a handsome grappler from Minnesota who had a neat crew cut and a muscular physique. Murphy beat Olson in thirty minutes and thirty seconds, securing his victory with his trademark move: a dropkick.

After the match, Murphy eventually returned to Medford, a densely settled residential suburb about five miles northwest of Boston. Medford occupied about eight square miles, and many of its streets were lined with triple-deckers and two-family homes. Its population had grown rapidly from 1915 to 1930, doubling to nearly sixty thousand in just fifteen years.

Murphy lived with his parents in a modest single-family house at 25 Saint Mary Street, in the eastern part of Medford, right on the border of the neighboring city of Malden. Across the street stood Immaculate Conception, the Catholic church where Murphy was baptized as a baby.

Dropkick Murphy had spent most of his life in Medford. That was his home. It was also a place where one of his dreams didn't come true.

Dropkick Murphy's father, James Daniel Murphy, was a tall, slender man with brown hair and blue eyes. Everyone called him Jimmy. He'd grown up in the neighboring city of Malden, and he made his living as a gas fitter, installing and repairing gas pipes and fixtures.

Dropkick Murphy's mother, Cicelie, was originally from Canada. She'd been born in Murray Harbor, a small fishing community on the southeastern coast of Prince Edward Island.

When Cicelie married Jimmy Murphy in 1911, she was twenty-four years old, living in Somerville and working as a tobacco stripper—an unglamorous occupation in which she mastered the tedious, monotonous task of peeling tobacco leaves from their stalks. Jimmy was twenty-six.

Their first and only child, John Eugene Murphy—a boy who would eventually become the pro wrestler known as Dropkick Murphy—was born on Tuesday, May 14, 1912. The family lived in Malden for the first eight years of his life. Just as Prohibition was getting underway, Jimmy and Cicelie Murphy moved out of Malden to an apartment in the neighboring city of Medford.

✽ ✽ ✽

Founded in 1630, Medford was one of the oldest English settlements in Massachusetts. The Mystic River flowed through the southern portion of the city, winding through low marshlands on a serpentine path until it joined the Malden River and then fed into Boston Harbor.

Early settlers found an abundance of clay deposits in Medford, which they used to make bricks, and the banks of the Mystic proved to be well-suited for building ships. But the most famous export to come out of Medford was rum.

Distilling liquor had been a big business in Medford since Colonial times. The biggest local producer of rum was the Lawrence family, whose company, Daniel Lawrence & Sons, oversaw the production of Old Medford Rum from 1824 until 1905 and made the brand famous. Made from molasses and advertised as "the best rum in the states," Old Medford Rum became a renowned brand that was recognized all over the country. It made its way into the names of cocktails (such as the Medford Sour, Medford Smash, Medford Rum Punch) and even a song (aptly titled "The Ballad of Medford Rum").

Bartending books specifically called for using Medford rum. Recipes for Medford Rum Punch appeared in bartender's guides from the 1860s all the way up through the 1930s.

MEDFORD RUM PUNCH
(Use a large bar glass.)
¾ tablespoonful of sugar
2 or 3 dashes of lemon juice, dissolve well with a little water
Fill the glass with fine shaved ice
1½ wine glass of Medford rum
Flavor with a few drops of Jamaica rum, stir up well and dress the top with fruit in season, and serve with a straw

After Daniel Lawrence & Sons shut down its distillery on Riverside Avenue in 1905, the Lawrence family sold the rights to Medford Rum (just the name—not the secret recipe) to M.S. Walker Inc., which kept the brand alive. Medford was still known for its rum, even though it was no longer made there.

But by the time Murphy was born, the three legacy industries that Medford was known for—shipbuilding, brickmaking, and rum distilling—had essentially disappeared. They were fields that he would have no future in.

✿ ✿ ✿

As a boy coming of age in Medford in the 1920s, Murphy experienced firsthand the explosive growth of football. High school football players were treated like heroes, and collegiate stars like the "Four Horsemen" of Notre Dame were national celebrities. Participation in the sport came to represent the epitome of toughness, manliness, and honor.

There was record-breaking attendance at college football games, and universities built bigger stadiums to accommodate the demand. High school football games drew huge crowds as well, as thousands of students, alumni, and spectators were more than willing to buy tickets to see the local boys play. Newspapers covered high school football games in great detail.

"Football crazy" is how *Boston Globe* writer Louis Lyons described the high school football scene of the 1920s. And Murphy's hometown of Medford was no different. It wasn't unheard of for thousands of fans to show up to watch the high school games.

Malden and Medford were fierce competitors on the gridiron. The two neighboring cities had a long-standing Thanksgiving Day rivalry that dated back to 1889. Every autumn, the anticipation would build throughout the high school football season, leading up to the big game on Thanksgiving Day, when the Medford's blue and white would take on Malden's blue and gold. It was an annual tradition.

Medford loved its high school football team, and like many other boys his age, Murphy hoped to play for Medford High one day. He was determined. He'd stop at nothing to be a football star.

✿ ✿ ✿

His father, Jimmy, introduced him to the sport of football at an early age. The elder Murphy knew the game well, but not in the conventional sense. Jimmy Murphy didn't play, and he wasn't a coach—he was a drum major.

For many years, he led the band that played at the annual Medford–Malden Thanksgiving football game.

As Johnny watched his dad in action, spinning his baton as he led the band, the football field became one of his favorite places to be.

For years, Malden's music dominated the stands at football games. But in the fall of 1925, when Johnny Murphy was thirteen years old, Medford High School organized a school band of its own. Johnny wasn't in high school yet—he was only in eighth grade—but he jumped at the opportunity to lead the newly formed band and show off the baton-twirling skills that his father had taught him.

On November 26, 1925, Medford's new high school band made its official debut at the Thanksgiving football game at the Fulton Street field. Leading the way was little Johnny Murphy, twirling his drum major's baton and tossing it high up into the air. His blue eyes looked upward, following the trajectory of the shiny metal stick against the blue sky, spinning round and round until it finally dropped back down into his hands.

He put on quite the show. The crowd of fifteen thousand clapped and cheered—they loved it.

Seated in the stands that day, among the thousands of fans, was Eugene G. McGillicuddy, a loyal alum of Medford High who worked as a cartoonist for the *Boston Globe*, drawing for the sports pages under his pen name, Gene Mack. He was a slim man with an impeccably steady hand, and a talent for seeing (and drawing) things like no one else could.

Every November, he'd go to Medford High's Thanksgiving Day football game and write a play-by-play story for the next day's paper, which was always accompanied by one of his famous pen-and-ink illustrations. From his vantage point in the stands that autumn day, Mack was impressed at how Murphy could twirl and catch the baton and pull off stunts so casually. The kid made it look easy.

Medford ended up losing the game that day, so Mack decided to pay homage to Johnny Murphy in his next cartoon. The cartoon appeared on page twenty-two of the *Boston Globe* the next day, where it was seen by thousands upon thousands of people. In the story that accompanied the cartoon, Mack described how Johnny Murphy made "a great hit with the fans by his clever manipulations of the drum major baton."

Usually Mack's schoolboy football cartoons focused on the action on the field. He had a knack for capturing highlights of tackles and passes and runs with his pen, and he was known to sketch the faces of the players who performed exceptionally well. This time, Johnny Murphy was in there, front and center, featured as a star in the cartoon, along with Mack's own words that summed up the day: "The only thing Medford won was the band leader's contest."

Johnny Murphy began ninth grade at Medford High School in the fall of 1926. He was already familiar with Medford High, since he was already a member of the band. To a youngster, Medford High was an imposing structure, three stories tall, made of brick and sandstone trim on a solid granite foundation. The school was located on Forest Street in Medford Square, the heart of the city, a star-shaped center where five main streets converged and trolley lines zigzagged against the sky. Streetcars rattled along the tracks, powered by a latticework of black electric wires overhead.

This little downtown area of Medford Square was home to Woolworth's, Medford Cafe, known for its coffee and homemade pastries, and P. Volpe & Sons, a corner market that sold fruits and vegetables. Kids would often take an apple and then scamper away, hoping and praying that "old man Volpe," who wore a straw hat, didn't see them stealing his precious fruit.

This was the Medford that Murphy knew as a young teenager.

The fall of his freshman year, Johnny joined Medford High's football team. The boys wore simple blue-and-white uniforms: baggy knickers, thick socks with stripes circling their lower legs, and jerseys with stripes circling their arms. Friction strips were sewn on the chest and inside of each arm. They were supposed to help the wearer keep a firm grip on the ball and prevent fumbles.

Medford had a strong team in the fall of 1926, with a lot of upperclassmen returning. As a fourteen-year-old freshman, Murphy was still small in size and didn't see much playing time. But Murphy couldn't stand being benched. Every game he watched from the sidelines was probably excruciating. After about a month of high school football, he had had enough. He decided he couldn't just stand outside in the cold anymore, watching his teammates running, throwing, and making tackles on the field. He needed to do something else.

That's when he decided to leave Medford's football team and take up a different extracurricular activity, something he'd been doing all along: He would join Medford High School's band instead. After he announced his intentions to his friends and family, the news of his decision made the pages of the *Boston Globe*.

"I'm quitting," Murphy told the *Globe*. "I can score more field goals with my baton than with a football."

There were twenty-seven boys in Medford High School's band that year. One played the oboe, one played the mellophone, one was on cymbals, one on trombone, and one on bass drum. There were seven saxophonists, six trumpet players, three drummers, three clarinetists, and two baritone players.

And there was one drum major. That was Johnny Murphy.

From that point on, he would no longer be stuck on the sidelines.

On Saturday, November 13, 1926, Medford High hosted Waltham High, a well-known football powerhouse. The captain of Waltham High's team was Tony Siano, a strong athlete with dark, wavy hair and a wide nose like a boxer's. The game remained scoreless until the fourth quarter, when Medford kicked a field goal to take the lead.

Murphy tried to boost the spirits of the crowd, but no amount of music or baton twirling could help his old teammates beat Waltham that day, as Medford ultimately succumbed to Siano's team, 7–3. But it wouldn't be the last time Murphy encountered Siano.

Unknown to anyone at the time, Murphy and Siano would meet again in the near future. But it would be under very different circumstances.

On Thanksgiving Day, November 28, 1929, readers of the *Boston Globe* were treated to another cartoon featuring Johnny Murphy. There, on the sports page, was an artist's rendition of Johnny twirling his baton and thrilling a cheering crowd. The headline above him read: "Medford Band Leader Puts on a Great Act; Johnny Murphy's Baton Whirling Would Make College Drum Major Jealous."

The accompanying article gushed about Murphy's talents. "Johnny can twirl a baton like nobody's business," Gene Mack wrote. "Johnny's evolutions would make many a college drum major look like a novice. He does everything except take live rabbits out of a derby hat . . . even the rival rooters look for his act as a big part of the day's program. He's a treat."

Murphy graduated from Medford High in 1930. In the high school yearbook, accompanying his senior year photo, was the quote: "As a leader of the band, he was the best in all the land."

Murphy's performance as the band leader did not go unnoticed by his classmates, and he received plenty of praise in the yearbook for his prowess at entertaining at the football games. "The Band, with Johnny Murphy and his twirling baton, received almost as lusty a cheer as the football squad," the yearbook stated.

But Murphy wanted to be noticed on the gridiron for other reasons. Despite his success with Medford High's band, Johnny Murphy still wanted to play competitive football. If he couldn't do it in Medford, he would try elsewhere.

3

OFF TO COLLEGE

*"Build up your weaknesses until they become
your strong points."*
—Knute Rockne

I n September 1930, Murphy said goodbye to his hometown and set
off for New Hampshire to attend Saint Anselm, a Catholic liberal
arts college founded by Benedictine monks in 1889. The campus was
located on a hilltop overlooking the city of Manchester. From the
top of the hill where Saint Anselm stood, Murphy could take in stunning
views. He could see the two peaks of the Uncanoonuc Mountains, and
vistas of pine trees, farmland, and orchards, as well as the Piscataquog
River, which fed into the Merrimack River.

It was a different world from home.

Murphy was now staying in a dormitory. Just like the rest of the young
men, who came from towns all over Massachusetts and New England and
beyond, he unpacked and settled in.

The centerpiece of St. Anselm was the main building, a Victorian structure that anchored the campus. The gymnasium at St. Anselm was relatively modern, having been built in 1911, and contained the typical fitness
equipment of the day: pulley weights, iron dumbbells, wooden dumbbells,
horizontal and parallel bars, rings, ropes, poles, vaulting horses, spring-
boards, mats, and Indian clubs, which were bowling pin–shaped weights
that people used to swing around to build strength in their shoulders,
back, and arms.

As an institution, St. Anselm promised to take a young man out of high
school and turn him into a "refined, college-bred gentleman."

The sports teams at St. Anselm were known as the Hilltoppers. Football had been an athletic tradition at Saint Anselm that dated back to 1894 (the St. Anselm football team defeated Boston College that year, 16–0). But football hadn't been a top priority at Saint Anselm for a while. At one point, in January 1915, school officials decided to drop the sport entirely.

But when Murphy arrived on campus in the fall of 1930, a major change was underway: Saint Anselm was trying to revive its athletic programs, starting with football. And they pinned their hopes on one man: Harry O'Boyle. A Notre Dame alumnus, he was brought in to turn things around at Saint Anselm. O'Boyle was hired to coach not only football, but also the basketball and baseball teams. O'Boyle signed a two-year contract to work at St. Anselm, and his first true test would be with the sport for which he was known best—football.

O'Boyle was an All-American football star from the Midwest. From a football standpoint, his resume was impressive. He had played for Notre Dame under legendary coach Knute Rockne. During his sophomore year, in 1924, he played the backfield and was one of Rockne's "Shock Troops"—a squad of second-string players who started certain games and played their hearts out, fighting for every millisecond of glory on the gridiron. After about five minutes or so, Rockne would take out the "Shock Troops" and send in his first-string players to finish the opposing team off.

O'Boyle became known as "one of Rock's fleetest halfbacks" and combined strength and speed with natural athletic ability. Rockne once said of the five-foot-nine O'Boyle: "He was what was known as a triple threat, being a good kicker, passer, and runner. His chief characteristics were determination and fight, counterbalanced with smartness, intellect, and headwork." O'Boyle went on to play for the Green Bay Packers.

But O'Boyle had always been realistic about football, and given his own personal experience, he knew the sacrifices that were needed to have a successful team. Some players would be relegated to limited roles. That was inevitable and part of the game. He knew this firsthand from his experience at South Bend. As he once said of his famous former teammates, the "Four Horsemen," "the Holy Ghost couldn't have broken into that lineup."

Officials at Saint Anselm were happy to hire O'Boyle. With such impressive football credentials, they believed O'Boyle could get the job done and—perhaps—bring Saint Anselm's out of the prep-school ranks and back to intercollegiate level, so they could go back to competing against old rivals like Boston College. That was something the school hadn't done in a long time.

On Saint Patrick's Day, March 17, 1930, a dinner was held in Manchester to welcome O'Boyle. It was attended by about a hundred coaches and alumni. Abbot Bertrand Dolan was the third president of St. Anselm and leading the college through a tough economic time. Dolan addressed everyone at the dinner, and when he introduced O'Boyle, he predicted a new start for athletics at St. Anselm. "Education and athletics can run side by side," said Dolan. "With careful management I see no reason why there cannot be further advancement in athletics which the American public so enthusiastically desires. I am with you to the limit, and if God gives me power, we'll drive on." The sports-minded audience applauded enthusiastically.

Murphy was one of 224 students attending Saint Anselm that fall. At that time, St. Anselm still had a prep school as well as a college that awarded Bachelor of Arts degrees.

Murphy was introduced to a new daily regimen at St. Anselm. Every hour, the bells high up in the cupola of the main building would ring, sending a familiar chime over the campus. Six days out of the week, the boys were woken up at 6 o'clock in the morning. Morning prayers and Holy Mass started at 6:30 sharp. This was followed by breakfast at 7 o'clock, and classes started at 7:30. Every evening, they went to bed (or at least they were supposed to) at 8:45 p.m.

On Sundays, they could sleep in an extra half-hour. They would wake up at 6:30 and then got to the High Mass and Sermon at 8:15. In the afternoon, they would return to the chapel at 3 o'clock for Vespers and Benediction.

Murphy earned a spot on the roster of St. Anselm's football team and quickly found himself immersed in the sights and sounds of the sport: The fresh smell of the grass and dirt from the field. The sound of the coach's whistle. The earthy scent of mud after a heavy rain. The aches in his muscles, and sting of scrapes and cuts on his arms and legs. The musty scent of football pads and leather helmets.

He found himself wearing the same colors that he wore in high school—blue and white. But that's where the similarities with Medford High ended. He was now playing alongside young men from all over Massachusetts.

He had teammates from Dorchester, Brockton, Cambridge, Marlborough, Holyoke, Falmouth, Springfield, Haverhill, and Palmer. Others came from Vermont, Maine, Pennsylvania, and Washington, D.C.

Murphy and his teammates wore leather helmets with aviator-style ear flaps. There were no face masks. His pants looked like baggy knickers, made of off-white canvas with a lace-up fly, reinforced knees, and a light layer of padding stitched into the thighs and hips. His cleats were high-top boots made of leather, rubber, and canvas. His jersey was a dark, heavy woolen sweater with friction strips stitched on the front—similar to the ones on the old Medford High uniforms. Murphy wore number seventy-seven.

O'Boyle taught Murphy and his teammates the plays and systems that he learned at Notre Dame. Or at least he tried to teach them. All the knowledge that he acquired while playing under Rockne over several seasons was difficult for the fresh-faced St. Anselm boys to absorb in a matter of days and weeks.

O'Boyle ran some tough practices. He spent hours showing the boys different formations, and walking through various plays, step-by-step, until they had memorized them perfectly. He ran drills and scrimmages. When some of the boys weren't living up to his expectations, he shifted people around to different positions. It was a tough time for the young coach and for his players.

After the team's first full practice game, a newspaper reporter asked O'Boyle what he thought about the strength of the team. O'Boyle had realistic expectations. If there weren't too many injures, he said, "we should have a fairly successful season."

St. Anselm got off to a good start: they defeated Samuel Johnson Academy, a prep school in Bridgeport, Connecticut, by a score of 26–0.

The next three games did not go as well. St. Anselm was beaten by Worcester Academy (6–0) and Phillips Exeter Academy (13–6), and two of their key starters were sidelined with injuries.

Murphy had not started in any games, but O'Boyle finally decided to give him a chance in a game against Vermont Academy on October 18. It was an away game, and the St. Anselm squad left on Friday at noon and traveled about two hours to Bellows Falls, Vermont, where they stayed overnight.

The Vermont Academy football team was a powerhouse, considered to be one of the top prep school teams in the East. The team had lost only one game since 1928, and thus far they were enjoying another undefeated season, having beaten St. Michael's College and the University of Vermont freshmen.

Murphy subbed in for the game against Vermont Academy, playing right end.

The Hilltoppers lost, 19–0. It was their third straight defeat. After the game, some of the boys were so distraught that they shed tears. For Murphy, the pain of losing may have been numbed somewhat by the new opportunity that was before him—he was finally getting playing time. Several Hilltoppers were out with injuries, and Murphy played well enough that he earned a spot on the first line at practice. O'Boyle then announced that Murphy would start in the next game against the Boston College freshman football team, known as the "Eaglets."

Boston College's student newspaper reported that the Eaglets appeared to be "the strongest frosh club ever assembled at the Heights" and the match was "expected to be one of the closest and hardest fought gridiron battles of the year."

Friday, October 24, 1930, was game day. It was raining. The field at Boston College was soaked. O'Boyle watched as his players slogged and sloshed around in the mud, scrambling for the ball. At times it was hard to distinguish the opposing sides because every jersey on the field was drenched and covered in mud. Their uniforms—made of canvas, wool, leather, and felt—absorbed the rainwater like a sponge and became heavier with every snap of the ball.

But the bad weather didn't seem to bother the rival star quarterback, Johnny Freitas. He was a talented Boston College freshman who was so quick and shifty that he earned the nickname "Snake Hips." The Hilltoppers couldn't stop Freitas as he carried the ball down the field and scored two touchdowns.

Saint Anselm lost, 19–2.

The only other team that Saint Anselm would beat that season was the freshmen team from Springfield College. The game was played at home in Manchester on Armistice Day, and two thousand fans attended. The American Legion and VFW were out in full force. There were fireworks and music supplied by two full bands. Murphy didn't start the game, but he got subbed in.

The Hilltoppers were trailing the Springfield College freshmen, by a score of 20–18, and the game was almost over. The Hilltoppers kept advancing upfield, reaching the twenty-five yard line. But their next two passing attempts failed. It was now fourth down. The ball was snapped, and Murphy, who was playing end, ran toward the end zone. The Hilltopper quarterback hurled the ball down the field, and Murphy made the catch at the nine-yard line. Then he was crushed by a tackle and taken down to the ground, his body slammed against the torn-up grass and dirt. But the football was still in his hands. His catch had secured a first down.

In the next play, a Hilltopper halfback pushed himself through the swarm of Springfield players until he went down at the four-yard line. The ball was snapped again, and a Hilltopper fullback scored the touchdown, giving St. Anselm's six points to win the game. The crowd went wild. The final score was 24–20. Murphy and his teammates felt great. It had been a close game, and they had worked hard for the win.

The last big game of the season would be held in Nashua, against Saint John's Preparatory School, a Catholic school for boys in Danvers, Massachusetts, that was favored to win the game.

On November 21, O'Boyle held their final practice of the year. After dinner, the marching band led all of the students through the campus. Students practiced cheers. O'Boyle stood before the students at the rally. Murphy and his teammates listened intently as the coach spoke.

"That team has the fight," yelled O'Boyle. "Have you?"

"It's all rosy when the team is winning," he said, as he looked around at his young charges. "But it is the real rooters that stick with it when it is losing."

The boys clapped and whistled. Then a huge bonfire was lit. Flames flickered and smoke billowed. Burning embers glowed bright orange. In the midst of the hooting and hollering, a group of students emerged from the darkness dragging a makeshift hearse and coffin that was supposed to represent the St. John's football team. The boys cheered even louder as the coffin was hoisted up and placed on top of the bonfire.

The following day, Murphy and his teammates boarded a bus and traveled twenty miles south to the city of Nashua, where they would face Saint John's. Saint Anselm also brought a lot of fans; the students and faculty rode in chartered buses.

The two teams met at the North Common before a crowd of three thousand people. Murphy trotted out onto the field. He had made the starting lineup, as one of the ends.

Also on the field that day was his old classmate from Medford High, Emilio "Big Ben" DeBenedictis, who stood over six feet tall and weighed 220 pounds. Big Ben towered over his teammates at St. John's. Murphy probably enjoyed seeing a familiar face out on the field. Murphy also knew to watch out for him.

Murphy went out on the field and did his job, but whatever fantasies he may have had about catching a long pass or breaking through St. John's defense to win the game would not come to fruition. Not one touchdown was scored, and their last game of the season ended in a tie, 0–0.

On Tuesday, December 9, a banquet was held for the Saint Anselm football team at the school's refectory in Manchester. St. Anselm's president, its athletic director, coaches, and other alumni and faculty took turns speaking to the room full of young men.

O'Boyle noted that many of his teammates wanted to return to play next year.

Murphy was one of twenty-four members of the football squad who were awarded letters that evening. It would also be his last. Two months later, he would leave Saint Anselm's for good. Why Murphy left St. Anselm's is unclear. But one thing is certain—Murphy didn't give up on his education or on his dream of playing football. In the autumn of 1931, he decided to do a postgraduate year at Bucksport Seminary, a coed college preparatory boarding school in Bucksport, Maine.

❈ ❈ ❈

Located in a small mill town on the Penobscot River, Bucksport Seminary was eighteen miles away from Bangor and about a ten-hour drive from Boston. The seventy-five-acre campus overlooked the river and featured a pine grove, tennis courts, and athletic fields. The school was founded in 1850 by the East Maine Conference of the Methodist Episcopal Church and was known for its strong athletic program. Murphy joined the football team and plodded through what could best be described as a mediocre season. Wet weather made for soggy fields that fall, and the team was plagued with injuries and a disappointing game schedule, as they didn't have many suitable opponents to play. In one scrimmage Bucksport beat a team 59–0 using their second-string linemen.

By the end of the season, Murphy was ready for a new challenge. He decided to take up a different sport for the winter—one that would change the course of his life.

It was at Bucksport that Murphy fell in love with wrestling.

The school's wrestling coach at the time was Lloyd Appleton, a wrestling star who had gone undefeated in college and won a silver medal in wrestling at the 1928 Olympics in Amsterdam. When Murphy arrived at the school, Appleton was still wrestling competitively and pursuing a spot on the 1932 Olympic team.

Murphy enjoyed wrestling. Unlike football, he didn't have a coach dictating when he could play, where he would run, and what he could do. When he wrestled, he was in control. Although he was part of a team, his fate was firmly in his own hands.

And he excelled. Murphy wasn't the only rookie wrestler on the team, as Appleton was coaching a squad full of newcomers. Only two veterans had returned to the team; the rest, like Murphy, were brand new. In February the Bucksport wrestlers traveled to Massachusetts to compete in a series of matches against collegiate teams. The first meet took place on Thursday, February 18, 1932, in his hometown of Medford, in a new gymnasium at Tufts College. Murphy wrestled in the 175-pound class and defeated his opponent handily in one minute and thirty-six seconds.

That season Murphy and his fellow Bucksport wrestlers would go on to compete against the freshmen teams at the Massachusetts Institute of Technology and Harvard.

But Murphy's time at Bucksport Seminary was short. He left the school in 1932. The following year, Bucksport Seminary filed for bankruptcy, and the school closed down for good. Murphy opted to return to Massachusetts and continue his studies closer to home. Having lived away from home for two years, he likely returned with a new sense of maturity and wisdom. He also had a new dream to pursue.

Murphy was interested in health and the human body and believed a career in medicine could be promising. He enrolled at the Massachusetts College of Osteopathy, located at 415 Newbury Street in the Back Bay section of Boston. Four years of schooling were required to earn a doctor of osteopathy degree. If he completed the coursework and passed the necessary exams, he would be a fully licensed physician, just like an MD, but with different initials: DO.

Practitioners of osteopathic medicine use a holistic approach to treat patients. Instead of focusing on a specific body part or organ system, DOs look at the person as a whole and provide care for the mind, body, and spirit. They also promote nutrition, exercise, and a healthy lifestyle as key to preventing disease.

While these may sound like modern concepts, they have been cornerstones of osteopathic medicine since the very beginning. ("DOs were holistic before holistic became cool," is how Dr. William Mayo, the past president of the American Osteopathic Association, once put it.) Today, in 2023, more than one in four medical students in the United States attends an osteopathic medical school, and osteopathic medicine is one of the fastest-growing healthcare professions in the country.

But that wasn't the case when Murphy entered medical school. Back then, there were only approximately six thousand DOs practicing in the United States. They represented about 4 percent of the physician population in the 1930s.

Osteopathy was still a relatively new field that only dated back to 1874. It was the brainchild of Dr. Andrew Taylor Still, a physician from Kirksville, Missouri, who came to believe that many modern medical practices of his time seemed to cause more harm than good. Born in a log cabin in Virginia, Still grew up hunting and farming and went on to become a frontier doctor who served in the Civil War. He lost his first wife due to childbirth complications in 1859, and five years later, he lost three of his children to spinal meningitis and a fourth child to pneumonia. After suffering these personal losses, he began questioning the practices of modern medicine and came to believe that doctors were overprescribing drugs. "Not until my heart had been torn and lacerated with grief and affliction could I fully realize the inefficiency of drugs," he wrote in his autobiography. "Some may say that it was necessary that I should suffer in order that good might come, but I feel that my grief came through gross ignorance on the art of the medical profession." He then made it his mission to come up with something better.

After the Civil War, Still began to realize that vast numbers of people were suffering from addiction. "By day and night I saw legions of men and women stagger to and fro, all over the land, crying for freedom from habits of drugs and drinks," he wrote.

With the war behind him, Still began looking at the world around him with a new perspective. Wherever he went, he was surrounded by Americans who were enslaved to drugs and alcohol. Still placed the blame on "the ignorance of our 'Schools of Medicine'" and the doctors themselves.

"I found that he who gave the first persuasive dose was also an example of the same habit of dosing and drinking himself, and was a staggering form of humanity, wound hopelessly tight in the serpent's coil," he said.

Still would eventually soften his tone toward traditional practitioners of what was then modern medicine. "I love the old doctors for their faithfulness; I pity them for their universal failure," he once said. "I know their intentions were good."

Still pressed on to find different methods of healing and developed new techniques that would change the practice of medicine in the United States forever. In 1892 Still founded the American School of Osteopathy in Missouri to teach his new system of medicine to the next generation of doctors. Instead of relying on alcohol or narcotics to cure ills, osteopathy was billed as a "drugless system of healing" that focused on the body's ability to heal itself.

The students at Still's medical school were trained to manipulate the patients' musculoskeletal system to relieve pain and treat certain ailments. They used pressure and resistance to move joints and muscles. Some of the movements were reminiscent of therapeutic massage and stretching.

Murphy would learn all about these natural remedies when he enrolled in the Massachusetts College of Osteopathy in the fall of 1932. When Murphy began his studies at the college, there were fifty registered physicians on the faculty, and students received eight hours of instruction a day. Lectures took place in the morning, starting at 8 a.m., and laboratory time, demonstrations, and clinics took place in the afternoon.

For nine months out of the year, from September to June, Murphy spent his days at the college, learning the principles of Dr. Andrew Taylor Still, taking courses in biology, histology, pathology, anatomy, physics, embryology, and surgery. It was there that he learned that Still, the founder of osteopathy, considered alcoholism to be an illness: "Drunkenness is no disgrace but is proof that the man has a disease," Still wrote in 1910.

Still disagreed that those who drank excessively lacked morals: "Is it disgrace for man to drink alcohol, brandy or whisky when he has great thirst for such drinks? Would it not be cruel to turn such patient away as though he were criminal and you would be disgraced to be seen in his company?"

It was during these classes that Murphy also learned about delirium tremens, a serious form of alcohol withdrawal that heavy drinkers often experienced after having their last drink. Symptoms included shaking and trembling, moodiness, confusion, and even hallucinations.

When treating alcoholism, osteopathic physicians treated each case individually, with a special focus on their nutrition. Back then DOs used several techniques on alcoholics. One treatment was to stretch the patient's neck. The patient would lie down on his back, and the osteopathic physician would place one hand under the patient's chin and the other at the base of his skull, and then gently pull on the patient's head until his body moved. Textbooks stated that this movement "frees the circulation in the neck and especially between the vertebrae of the entire spine."

Another treatment called for the DO to take the patient's leg and bring it up to the patient's chest, stretching the leg muscles. There were also treatments where the physician would apply pressure to the patient's liver, stomach, and spleen.

Murphy did not know it yet, but he would draw upon those lessons later in his life.

In the fall of 1935, the Massachusetts College of Osteopathy relocated to 473 Beacon Street in the Back Bay, an elegant brownstone building that had just been remodeled. It is here that Murphy spent his final year finishing his course of studies.

Murphy was not the only student who was working his way through school. But it's safe to say he was one of the few—if not the only—professional wrestlers at the college. His ultimate goal was to become a doctor, and moonlighting on the wrestling circuit helped pay for his medical school tuition. He attended classes, participated in clinics, and worked in the laboratories. He scribbled down notes while listening to lectures, forgetting about the scraped elbows and knees and welts and bruises he received while wrestling the night before.

4

WRESTLING LIFE

"There's no drama like wrestling."
—Andy Kaufman

W restling is widely recognized as the world's oldest sport. For as long as human beings have walked the Earth, they have battled against each other in one-on-one contests of strength, fitness, and domination. Wrestling became an event in the ancient Olympic Games in 708 BCE.

In the late 1800s, archaeologists stumbled across an 18-inch-wide piece of papyrus in Egypt. The ancient document contained instructions on how to wrestle that were written in Greek in the second century. It described how to sweep the legs of your opponent, how to put him in a headlock, and how to throw him.

Some wrestling events—even way back then, in ancient times—were fixed. Evidence of fakery can be found in another text discovered in Egypt dating back to 267 CE. Professor Dominic Rathbone of King's College London translated the document, which describes how one wrestler promises to "fall three times and yield" to his opponent in exchange for 3,800 drachmas (a form of Greek currency). *Smithsonian Magazine* called it "the first known bribery contract in ancient sports."

And thus, perhaps rightfully so, wrestling has always been watched closely by skeptics. After all, it's a lot easier to coordinate a victory or loss in a contest between two people rather than a team sport that requires multiple competitors.

Fast-forward to the nineteenth century, when traveling carnivals were a popular form of entertainment in the United States. Many carnivals featured "Athletic Shows," commonly known as "AT shows," in which a boxer or wrestler employed by the carnival would challenge spectators to take on anyone in the audience. Often a coworker would be planted in the audience and volunteer to fight. Unbeknownst to the audience, that person was also employed by the carnival. The whole thing was scripted. Bets would be placed, and, as you can guess, the carnival pocketed the winnings. The people who put on the AT shows knew how to get the crowds worked up.

That's where Jackie Nichols, one of Dropkick Murphy's regular opponents, got his start. "In those days, the fairs always had an athletic show," Nichols said in an interview with the *Bangor Daily News*. "They'd have a wrestler who would take on all challengers. The challengers would get a dollar a minute for as long as they could last. I decided I'd wrestle the guy at the Windsor Fair. Then I went to the Litchfield Fair, then to the Topsham Fair. I earned $300 that summer."

Many early pro wrestlers started out on the carnival circuit and brought with them their techniques and expertise of "working" fights to make them appear to be real. This only pushed the sport further into a different realm, away from actual competition and more toward spectacle and entertainment.

In March 1910, the *New York Times* reported that professional wrestlers and promoters were accused of encouraging betting on rigged matches to win money as well as using packets of fake blood in fixed matches. The *Times* reported that one professional wrestler from Michigan testified how "a bladderful of blood was caused to burst in his opponent's mouth at a critical moment as a ruse" to stop a match.

Throughout Dropkick Murphy's career, matches were almost always planned in advance. Lou Thesz, who started wrestling professionally in the 1930s, wrote about this in his acclaimed memoir, *Hooker*, in which he explained how wrestlers discussed how the match would play out in the dressing room and communicated with each other in the ring.

"What we did in the ring comes closest to being described as a strenuous form of extemporaneous theater," wrote Thesz.

In his memoir, Thesz recalled that back then it was still possible to see a legitimate contest once in a great while, but those occasions grew increasingly rare. On top of that, the overall lack of organization in wrestling meant there was no clear way of holding a national championship.

Different promoters had carved out and claimed different territories around the country and continued to award championship belts to whomever they saw fit—or, more important, to whomever suited their business needs.

When Dropkick Murphy started wrestling professionally, Boston's most powerful wrestling promoter was Paul F. Bowser. A former wrestler himself, Bowser was married to the famous female wrestler Cora Livingston. Bespectacled and savvy, Bowser set up the biggest wrestling matches that Boston had ever seen.

One of those matches took place on June 29, 1928, between two of the biggest wrestling stars of the day: "Dynamite" Gus Sonnenberg and Ed "Strangler" Lewis.

Born on March 6, 1898, in Ewen, a small community in the Upper Peninsula of Michigan, Sonnenberg had been an All-American tackle at Dartmouth and later played in the NFL. But Sonnenberg eventually left professional football to embark on a career in professional wrestling. He quickly gained fame in the wrestling ring for his "flying tackle" move, in which he would put his head down and rush at his opponents. If the move worked in his favor—as it usually did—he'd smash into his rival's midsection and knock him clear off his feet.

Sonnenberg became a big-name celebrity and a top attraction, and went on to earn many nicknames, including "Dynamite Gus," "Sonny," and, most notably, "The Goat," because of the way he'd lower his head and charge at his opponents.

When Sonnenberg faced Ed "Strangler" Lewis at Boston Arena, he was thirty years old and still new to wrestling. Lewis was three inches taller and at least twenty-five pounds heavier than Sonnenberg. He was an icon of the ring, and one day away from his thirty-seventh birthday.

A crowd of twelve thousand fans packed into the legendary auditorium to watch the two wrestlers compete for the heavyweight title. By all accounts, the match was a financial success.

Bowser scheduled the two wrestling stars to meet again on January 4, 1929, at the newly built Boston Garden, which had been open for less than two months. The match drew a sellout crowd.

Sitting in a draped box-seating area directly behind Sonnenberg were Massachusetts Governor Frank Allen, his wife, and his mother-in-law. Others in the crowd included drug-store kingpin Louis K. Liggett, former Boston Mayor John "Honey Fitz" F. Fitzgerald, and General Edward L. Logan, the man for whom Boston's airport would later be named.

Massive movie cameras in the west balcony were pointed down toward the ring, capturing the action on film.

During one of the preliminary bouts, one overenthusiastic fan could be heard shouting, "Just paralyze that arm. Break it off and give it to me for a souvenir. I'll give you twenty dollars for it!"

Sonnenberg charged like a bull at Lewis, headbutting him in the stomach. Lewis landed on his back. Sonnenberg scored the first fall. The fans went wild, throwing hats and papers. Sportswriter David F. Egan covered the match for the *Boston Globe* and described the visceral reaction that Sonnenberg drew from the audience. "The crowd went into conniption fits when he scored the first fall," Egan wrote.

Sonnenberg continued his assault, knocking Lewis out of the ring several times. The last time, the referee reached the count of ten before Lewis climbed back into the ring, disqualifying him, which meant the diamond-studded championship belt went to Sonnenberg. Billy Sandow, Lewis's manager, jumped into the ring and began arguing with the referee. But the decision stood: Gus was the new heavyweight champ.

It was front-page news the next day. The *Globe* reported that more than twenty thousand fans attended the event, which brought in a record amount of money at the gate.

Bowser booked Sonnenberg and Lewis to meet once again in Boston—this time, at Fenway Park on July 9, 1929. The *Boston Globe* reported that Sonnenberg would receive $75,000—the largest paycheck for any wrestler in the history of the sport.

Sonnenberg opened the doors for many other college athletes and showed them that good money could be made in pro wrestling. In the years to come, many other collegiate football players jumped from the gridiron to the so-called "squared circle." They included "Jumping" Joe Savoldi from Notre Dame; Ed Don George from the University of Michigan; "Bibber" McCoy from Holy Cross; John "Kewpie" Kilroy from

Boston College; Bronko Nagurski, an All-American from the University of Minnesota; and Jim McMillen, an All-American from the University of Illinois who went on to play for the Chicago Bears.

This wave of collegians proved to be popular among the fans and a boon to promoters. But syndicated sports columnist Robert Edgren was not impressed. In 1931, the writer lamented that many of these newcomers lacked real wrestling skills. "College football heroes are rushed into the mat game . . . without knowing much of what it's all about," Edgren wrote, "as long as their football reputations can be capitalized."

When John Murphy saw so many collegiate football players going into pro wrestling, perhaps he thought, *maybe I can do that, too*. According to one newspaper account, Murphy witnessed his first pro wrestling match in 1932, and Gus Sonnenberg was one of the headliners. From that point on, Murphy watched as many Sonnenberg bouts as he could, and even visited the gym where he trained. And thus began his foray into the secretive world of professional wrestling.

Murphy's good looks and athletic build, combined with his academic pedigree, made him an attractive recruit to promoters like Charlie Gordon. Gordon was an enterprising promoter in Boston but always seemed to be scrambling for business; he could never catch up with the indomitable Paul Bowser. Gordon put on Tuesday night shows at the Mechanics Building. He also booked shows at other venues around Massachusetts, such as the Crescent Rink in Lowell, and even an occasional match at Fenway Park and the Boston Opera House. When Gordon first started booking Murphy for matches, he hoped that he could develop into a dependable box-office draw.

Promoters worked hard to build stables of wrestlers that they could rely on to bring in audiences week after week. Throughout the Great Depression, promoters did just about anything they could to lure paying customers through the turnstiles. They held battle royals. Mud-wrestling matches and cage matches. Wrestling matches in a ring full of tomatoes. Tag team matches and matches in snow. Blindfolded matches and matches in ice cream. One Boston promoter, Steve McPherson, offered anyone the chance to attend a show for free on an I.O.U. and pay him later. Fans just needed to show up with a valid ID in lieu of cash. And they did, bringing their driver's licenses, lodge cards, and auto registrations. One fan brought his divorce papers to prove his identity.

Indeed, pro wrestling was different from any other sport.

"It isn't sport; it is show business," said wrestling promoter Jack Pfefer in a 1938 interview with *Collier's* magazine. "I'm not an athletic promoter; I'm a theatrical man. Like Ziegfield or the Shuberts maybe. I don't tell people my wrestling shows are on the level; I guarantee them they're not. I've never seen an honest wrestling bout in my twenty years in the game. Maybe there was one, but I wasn't there. And I'd hate to see one, it'd be an awful thing!"

It was true: to a casual observer, amateur wrestling could be boring to watch. Two men would lock each other in holds and could stay in the same position for a while. With so little movement, those matches seemed to drag on and on. Matches like that weren't drawing people in. People wanted to see a show.

The world of professional wrestling in the 1920s and 1930s provided action-packed entertainment, full of nonstop movement and drama. Both promoters and wrestlers shared two common goals: make money and thrill every audience. Get the fans pumped up, and most important of all, get them to come back. Colorful personalities and acrobatic moves came into vogue in professional wrestling. They excited the crowds.

To achieve the most action in the ring, and to build as much excitement in the seats as possible, most matches were choreographed and the winners selected ahead of time. There were plenty of theatrics and gimmicks in the ring. Professional wrestling had evolved into theatrical combat—a mix of drama, acrobatic showmanship, and athletic endurance.

Pfefer put it this way: "My fellows are tumblers, acrobats, like circus performers. They throw each other around, up in the air, out of the ring. They land on concrete floors or spectators' laps. But they seldom get hurt, and when they do it is an accident. They have rehearsed how to take those falls, y'understand, and they do it nearly every night in the week."

Outcomes would almost always be determined in advance. Wrestlers communicated in the ring in all sorts of ways. Often veteran wrestlers would lead the way and "call" the matches in the ring.

If a wrestler was going to punch a referee, the ref would typically be given the heads-up beforehand. But, as in any human endeavor, there were occasional mishaps. A ref, for example, might forget to duck and get socked in the face. Or a wrestler would get tossed from the ring, land awkwardly, and injure himself.

Although much of the action was staged, pro wrestlers often suffered serious injuries. Some even proved to be fatal (there were ten wrestling deaths in 1936, according to *Life* magazine). The occupational hazards of working in the ring resulted in broken bones, dislocated joints, sprained tendons and ligaments, and pulled muscles. Many wrestlers—including Ed "Strangler" Lewis—contracted trachoma, a contagious bacterial eye infection that caused blindness. Skin infections were even more common. "Cauliflower ear," a condition that results from blunt force trauma to the ear, was also extremely prevalent among wrestlers. Winn Robbins ended up with cauliflower ear after he found himself on the receiving end of a head-scissors move by Steve Passas, who used his legs to clamp down on Robbins's head and squeezed so hard that the skin separated from the cartilage in his ear, leaving him with a deformed ear. Cauliflower ear was viewed as a badge of honor among boxers and wrestlers. Robbins said the constant pounding wrestlers' bodies endured every night only made them tougher and made it so that "the blows give only a dull pain, and hurt us less than they would an average person."

Even though the risks of wrestling were, in fact, very real, the authenticity of wrestling as a real competition was questioned on a regular basis.

In December 1931 nationally syndicated columnist Robert Edgren penned a scathing column that castigated the state of professional wrestling. "A modern 'wrestling match' is purely a circus performance, a carefully planned series of stunts, laughable or startling, with the 'winner' of each fall scheduled in advance," he wrote. "It isn't a contest and it isn't on the level, except as a bit of entertainment."

The following week, Frank M. Smith responded to Edgren's column by writing a letter that was published in the *Boston Globe*. Smith was secretary of the Bay State Wrestling Association, the organization that represented local wrestling promoters in Massachusetts, and he blasted Edgren for making those accusations.

"The article, as written by Mr. Edgren, carries the implication that there isn't a wrestling contest being staged any place in the whole world at the present time that is not 'fixed,'" wrote Smith. "Nothing is farther from the truth. Mr. Edgren libels the sport of wrestling. There is no doubt that in backwoods places there are some discredited wrestlers who are staging entertainments instead of wrestling contests. The American Wrestling Association has no excuse to offer for these barnacles any more than the National Bankers Association will excuse an absconding member or church people will forgive an erring clergyman. For years I have followed and kept in close touch with the wrestling sport and would be the last one to tolerate any condition that Mr. Edgren would have the public believe now rules the sport."

Smith didn't have to worry. The believers continued to believe.

To be successful in the ring, Murphy had to employ techniques used by professional stuntmen. He practiced how to fall without getting injured. Through his early experiences in the ring, he learned how to get the audience going by pulling off acrobatic moves and exaggerating his facial expressions. He also began to understand the importance of good chemistry and choreography.

Murphy studied and rehearsed different wrestling moves and holds. Arm bar. Airplane spin. Body scissors. Double wrist lock. Head scissors. Flying mare. Hammerlock. Piledriver. Half nelson. Quarter nelson. Toehold. Wing lock.

One particular maneuver that he practiced often, and became his specialty, was, of course, the dropkick.

Murphy also had to learn to keep himself safe. Wrestling matches were rowdy events, and hostile fans tended to throw things. All sorts of things. Peanuts and other projectiles would rain down on wrestlers as they tussled inside the ring. Newspapers fluttered down from the balconies. Wrestlers would get pelted by paper clips and lit cigarettes. Airborne bottles would occasionally smash and break on the cement, leaving shards of shattered glass on the sawdust-covered floor surrounding the ring.

Things got so out of control at the Boston Garden that in April 1932, Dick Dunn, the vice president and general manager of the Garden, had had enough. Wrestling fans had to stop throwing bottles and trash around during matches. Dunn wrote an open letter that was published in the *Boston Globe*:

> I think that all fans should be their own policemen, and they should not only refrain from hurling missiles, but should also report to the

management any case of throwing on the part of anyone near them. The Boston Garden directors have spent thousands of dollars to properly police the Boston Garden and to see that their patrons are properly protected and have done everything to eliminate rowdyism in all its phases. If the fans of Boston will cooperate with us, we are sure that this throwing of missiles can be eliminated.

Dunn's public commentary may have had little effect on ringside behavior. But it definitely intrigued many young men, especially those who had never attended a live wrestling match.

Many professional wrestlers used stage names. Promoters would often embellish their credentials or concoct a completely fictional biography to pique the interest of fans.

During the Depression years, many pro wrestlers were cast to play roles as ethnic heroes, and Dropkick Murphy was one of them. Wrestlers at that time typically fell into one of two categories: the good guys, who in wrestling parlance were known as "babyfaces" or "faces," and the villains, known as "heels." Their nicknames and stage personalities would often reflect racial and ethnic stereotypes.

There was Dean Detton, aka the "Mormon Flash," from Salt Lake City. There was the German aristocrat Count Von Zuppe, who was marketed as a "Nazi matman" and "arch badman from Berlin." He wore his black hair slicked back, a top hat, monocle on his right eye, and a bright-red iron cross sewn on his satin robe. There was Zimba "Gorilla" Parker, who was billed as an "Ethiopian savage" and the "Brown Bomber." Ali Baba, a broad-shouldered, bald-headed brute with a thick handlebar mustache was marketed as the "Arabian sheik," even though he was actually Armenian and a U.S. Navy veteran.

Long before Jackie Robinson broke the color line of major league baseball, and before racial segregation ended in other professional sports, athletic showmen of all races worked the professional wrestling circuit. In fact, one of the first professional wrestlers to compete in this country was African American: a former enslaved man named Viro Small toured around New England wrestling under the name "Black Sam" in the nineteenth century. Small ended up making a name for himself as a pro in New York City, despite facing discrimination because of the color of his skin and other setbacks, including being shot in the neck. Small survived and continued to wrestle months later. The shooter was only sentenced to a year and a half in prison.

As early as 1935, Dropkick Murphy was wrestling on cards with Bill Parker, who wrestled under the stage names "Zimba Parker" and "Tiger Parker," and Jimmy "The Black Panther" Mitchell, a popular and pioneering Black wrestler from the South who, in the early years of his career, wore a mask when he wrestled.

One of Murphy's regular opponents was Kaimon Kudo, a popular Japanese-born wrestler who used judo moves and jiu-jitsu in the ring. In early 1938 Dropkick Murphy wrestled a series of matches against Kaimon Kudo at the New York Hippodrome, a venue located on Sixth Avenue in midtown Manhattan.

Another one of Murphy's opponents was Jack Claybourne, one of the most successful African American wrestlers of his time. A native of Missouri, Claybourne was two years older than Murphy and was a recognized champion in not only the United States but also Mexico, Australia, New Zealand, and Canada. He also had a devastating dropkick. On January 8, 1944, readers who picked up a copy of *The Afro-American*, a newspaper based out of Baltimore, saw two very different stories in the sports section. One story had the headline "Orioles Won't Use Colored Players." On the same page, another article told the story of how Jack Claybourne, the "Hub city mat sensation," beat Dropkick Murphy and "stole the limelight" before a capacity crowd at Boston Arena. That headline proudly declared: "Hub City Mat Shows New Grunt Luminary."

❧ ❧ ❧

Several flamboyant personalities emerged in the 1930s, such as Lord Patrick Lansdowne, who wore a monocle and was always accompanied by his butlers: Tweedles, Twittles, and Jeeves. The regal anthem "God Save the King" would blare from auditorium speakers every time he entered the ring. Although he masqueraded as snobby British royalty, the curly haired monocle-wearing wrestler was actually from Ohio. He developed his campy character over time and took his snootiness to a new level by bringing a teacup to his lips, and sipping tea, with his pinky finger extended out, in between falls. His wardrobe included a purple velvet robe, a black velvet cape lined with gold material, and a black tunic. A masterful showman, Lansdowne knew how to toy with the audience's emotions. He would often order his assistants to spray the mat with perfume or sanitizer before he entered the ring. His valets would kneel down, examine the mat closely, make a face, and then squeeze the bulb of the atomizer, spritzing a fine mist so the space would be suitable for their boss. Lansdowne took his time getting ready and would purposely remove his robe as slowly as possible, and then proceed to fold it as slowly as possible, building up tension in the audience.

Another colorful character from the 1930s was Sterling "Dizzy" Davis. He was from Houston, Texas, and crafted an effeminate stage presence, wearing kimonos and throwing gardenias to his fans. He wore his dark hair slicked back and a zebra-striped robe that had padded shoulders, oversized black cuffs, and his initials "D. D." emblazoned on the collar.

The flashy behavior and appearance of Dizzy Davis and Lord Lansdowne pioneered a new genre of dandy-like wrestling stars, the most famous of whom was Gorgeous George.

"Gorgeous" George Wagner was a childhood friend of Dizzy Davis. When he learned how the crowds would react to David's flower gimmick, George asked if he could try tossing orchids. He did, and it drove the fans crazy. Gorgeous George grew his hair out, so it was long and curly, and bleached his locks blond. Gold-plated bobby pins held his carefully coiffed hairdo together. His effeminate, pompous behavior elicited loud boos from the crowd.

When Gorgeous George appeared at wrestling shows, he would be accompanied by a loyal assistant who served as his personal valet. Dressed in a suit and bow tie, his valet looked like a butler and would dutifully inspect the mat and spray it down with perfume before George had to step through the ropes. Some curious observers would inquire what exactly was in the mysterious mist. To this question George would reply: "Chanel Number 10." When people asked, "You mean Chanel Number 5?" He would say, "No. Ten. Why be half safe?"

Before the match the valet would often carefully take the bobby pins off his platinum head, and with a flick of the wrist, George would toss them out to his loyal fans. Those bobby pins—or "Georgie pins" as he called them—became coveted souvenirs. He was even known to make some lucky recipients take an oath: "I solemnly swear and promise to never confuse this gold Georgie pin with a common, ordinary bobby pin, so help me Gorgeous George."

Professional wrestlers strived to make themselves stand out. Promoters encouraged this, too. For wrestling promoter Jack Pfefer, wrestlers' appearances were extremely important. The stranger they looked, the better. "Freaks I love and they're my specialty," Pfefer said. "I am very proud of some of my monstrosities. You can't get a dollar with a normal-looking guy, no matter how good he can wrestle. Those birds with shaved, egg-shaped heads, handlebar mustaches, tattooed bodies, big stomachs—they're for me!"

Pfefer's stable of grapplers included King Kong, a 635-pound former sideshow circus act named Martin Levy. Pfefer encouraged his wrestlers to use fake blood (a capsule of beet juice, hidden in their mouth) during matches, and even provided sneezing and itching powder for them to use on their opponents, a comical move that always got laughs from the audience.

Most popular wrestlers had a memorable nickname and a backstory that appealed to fans.

Murphy had no real need to concoct a fake biography: He was an honest-to-goodness former college football player who was wrestling professionally to put himself through medical school, and he had a catchy stage name too.

Unfortunately, there is no written record or historical evidence that explains just how John Murphy took on the nickname "Dropkick Murphy."

In his early matches, Murphy was billed as a former college football player (which he of course was). And back then, the word "dropkick" was a term commonly associated with football. Murphy was an active, energetic wrestler who was quick on his feet. His legs were strong and his body was agile, and he wanted to wow the audience.

It's not surprising that Dropkick Murphy chose a nickname associated with football, or that he chose to master one of the more difficult moves and, quite literally, make it his own.

The word "dropkick" originated in the nineteenth century. According to Merriam-Webster, the word first appeared in 1857 and it means "a kick made by dropping a ball to the ground and kicking it at the moment it starts to rebound."

The word has appeared in different variations, sometimes as one word, sometimes as two (drop kick) and sometimes with a hyphen (drop-kick). In the United States, the term was first associated with the game of football. In *Walter Camp's Book of College Sports*, published in 1893, Camp delves into the rules of football and defines a "drop-kick" as "letting the ball fall from the hands and kicking it at the very instant it rises."

The dropkick is still in the rule books of the NFL and NCAA, but it is rarely used. Its heyday was the early days of football. In 1925 newspapers ran instructions on how to perform a dropkick properly. In the 1930s, footballs became longer, slimmer, and more pointed at the ends, which made throwing and passing easier but made dropkicks even more difficult to execute. (The last time a dropkick was used successfully in the NFL was when New England Patriots quarterback Doug Flutie pulled one off on New Year's Day in 2006. The last successful NFL dropkick before that was in 1941.)

It wasn't until the Great Depression that the dropkick became a popular wrestling move. One of the early practitioners of the maneuver was Abe Coleman, a wrestler known as the "Hebrew Hercules" and "Jewish Tarzan" who started wrestling professionally in the late 1920s. Coleman claimed that he learned how to kick with two feet by watching kangaroos after traveling to Australia in 1930; he then made it his specialty. Early press accounts credit him with introducing "kangaroo kicks" to wrestling.

"Jumping Joe" Savoldi was another wrestler from the 1930s who popularized the dropkick in wrestling. Savoldi had been a star fullback for Notre Dame and played a key role on Knute Rockne's undefeated teams in 1929 and 1930. But his collegiate career was cut short when word got out that he was married and had filed for divorce, which led to his expulsion from Notre Dame. He went on to play in the NFL for the Chicago Bears before making his wrestling debut in 1931, and soon thereafter he adopted the flying dropkick as his signature move. Savoldi would jump up, kick his opponent with both feet, and then fall backward, with his rear end usually hitting the canvas. It was a tough move to pull off, but he managed to do it over and over again.

John "Dropkick" Murphy also made the move his own, perfecting it to a point that he could kick someone in the face with both boots and still land on his feet.

Dr. John "Dropkick" Murphy posing in front of a billboard
bearing his name on May 30, 1934. *Courtesy of David Murphy*

Dropkick Murphy
wrestled against athletes
of all races, including
Japanese-born wrestler
Kaimon Kudo (left),
long before racial
barriers were broken
in other pro sports.
*Courtesy of
David Murphy*

John "Dropkick" Murphy started wrestling professionally in the 1930s. *Courtesy of David Murphy*

Dropkick Murphy's business card. *Courtesy of David Murphy*

John "Dropkick" Murphy
with his first wife, Marie.
Courtesy of David Murphy

The Great Mephisto.
Courtesy Scott Teal/
Crowbar Press

Early on in their careers Paul Bowser and his wife Cora Livingston
wrestled at athletic shows on the carnival circuit, taking on all comers.
Courtesy of Scott Teal/Crowbar Press

BOWSER
PITTSBURGH'S
WRESTLING WONDER
$10.00 TO ANY MAN
HE FAILS TO THROW
IN TEN MINUTES.

George Dusette.
Courtesy Scott Teal/
Crowbar Press

Jackie Nichols.
Courtesy Scott Teal/
Crowbar Press

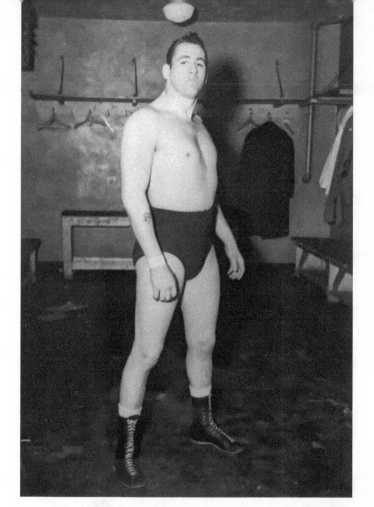

Ted Germaine.
*Courtesy Scott Teal/
Crowbar Press*

Dropkick Murphy lifts
a heavy log. *Courtesy
of David Murphy*

Dropkick Murphy shows how training was done back in the day, swinging an axe and chopping wood. *Courtesy of David Murphy*

The big red barn was the social hub of Bellows Farm. *Courtesy of David Murphy*

5

THE POLITICS OF GRAPPLING

All that's left now for the wrestlers to do is to go at each other with axes. Yes, axes! Place an ax in each wrestler's corner and give him the right to use it. . . . I'm told that this thing is permitted because the people want it. Suppose the people wanted to see murder—should we permit it?
—Maryland State Senator Joseph L. Donovan, November 1932

Professional wrestling was on the top of many people's minds in Boston on June 11, 1929. That morning, a photo of Gus Sonnenberg appeared across the front page of the *Boston Herald*. "Wrestling for Titles Great Flim Flam Game," read the headline. The lengthy story denounced wrestling as being "the greatest gold-brick industry in the history of modern sport." It was all a sham, according to the *Herald*. Pro wrestling matches were rehearsed, winners were picked beforehand, and there were so many different "champions" it was hard to keep track of them all.

Abraham B. Casson was convinced that something needed to be done. The twenty-nine-year-old legislator was one of the youngest members of the Massachusetts House of Representatives, and he saw an opportunity to capitalize on all the bad publicity around wrestling. On the day that the *Herald* story came out, as Casson headed to work, the weather was warm and pleasant, and the sun shone off the golden dome of the State House. It was a big day for Casson; this was the day he filed legislation to regulate wrestling in Massachusetts. It was a move that would have ramifications for the rest of his life and shape the rest of his career.

Despite concerns about its authenticity, professional wrestling still proved to be popular. During the Great Depression, it was drawing bigger box-office returns than boxing or any other sport, with the exception of baseball.

Thanks in part to football stars like Gus "The Goat" Sonnenberg and savvy promoters like Paul Bowser, pro wrestling in the United States enjoyed something of a renaissance in the late 1920s and early '30s. Daily newspapers carried regular coverage of wrestling, and even though many observers questioned the validity of the contests, people continued to come out to watch the shows.

Wrestling matches were typically rowdy affairs. Spectators screamed until their voices went hoarse. Chairs and bottles were thrown. Referees got punched. Fans started brawls. Police were called in to stop matches. Wrestlers would try all sorts of dirty tricks in the ring, much to the delight of the audience. Some threw chairs at each other or used the ropes to strangle their opponents. During one exciting bout, a woman at ringside became so emotional that she smashed the neck off of a glass Coca-Cola bottle and went after one of the wrestlers with it. Sometimes it was difficult to tell what was fake and what was real.

Wrestling was viewed as a wild, anything-goes type of business, which led to some calling for its regulation. And there was another thing: Wrestling was bringing in lots of cash, and like any other moneymaking activity, the government started taking notice. Politicians began to view the sport as a potential source of revenue.

There had been efforts to regulate wrestling throughout the 1920s. In May 1921, New York Governor Nathan L. Miller signed a bill that put professional wrestling under the supervision of the New York State Athletic Commission. Within months, the commission had banned four wrestling moves—strangleholds, toeholds, scissors, and headlocks—from wrestling matches held in New York. Scratching, striking, gouging, and "any display of bad temper" were also prohibited, and any grappler guilty of committing such infractions would be disqualified and have their license revoked. A *New York Times* article made the amusing prediction that if the new rules were enforced as written, "future bouts in this state should be thoroughly genteel affairs."

In June 1923, Pennsylvania enacted a similar law and created a state commission to oversee wrestling and boxing. It also allowed the state to collect 5 percent of gross receipts as well as annual license fees from the participants.

Indeed, soon enough, other states began to follow New York and Pennsylvania's lead. Bills to regulate wrestling popped up all across the country, in places like Louisiana, Oklahoma, California, West Virginia, Colorado, Ohio, and Illinois.

Casson thought it was time that Massachusetts took action.

Under Casson's proposed plan, professional wrestling in Massachusetts would fall under the jurisdiction of the state boxing commission. Casson argued that wrestling had become so popular that police and fire protection were necessary at matches, and that wrestling promoters should be required to chip in their fair share to cover the costs of protecting the public.

But he wasn't the only Massachusetts legislator pushing to regulate wrestling—several other lawmakers filed similar bills. Representative Slater Washburn of Worcester petitioned for a special commission to investigate boxing and wrestling in Massachusetts, to see what, if any, new regulations should be implemented. Casson spoke in favor of Washburn's proposal.

During one contentious hearing at the State House, Washburn declared that wrestling in Massachusetts was "one of the best rackets of the present time."

Former lieutenant governor Edward P. Barry took issue with that statement.

"That isn't so!" Barry shouted. "You are now saying that most of the wrestling bouts are not on the level. You didn't say that at previous hearings, and you know it isn't so."

Washburn turned to the audience and reminded them that Barry was no longer a public servant in an elected office—he was working for Paul

Bowser now. The former lieutenant governor was the legal counsel for the most powerful wrestling promoter in Boston.

Casson's bill got plenty of publicity, which instantly raised his profile on Beacon Hill.

As Casson sought to regulate professional wrestling in Massachusetts, the state of New York continued to tighten its grip on the sport. In April 1930, the New York State Athletic Commission ruled that all professional wrestling events should be called "shows" or "exhibitions," and they could no longer be advertised as "contests" or "matches." This decision was made after Commissioner William Muldoon, former fighter and celebrity trainer, conducted an investigation into New York's wrestling scene.

On May 19, 1930, Massachusetts Governor Frank G. Allen decided to follow New York's example and signed a bill to create a special commission to investigate boxing and wrestling in the Bay State. The panel would include a senator, three state representatives, and three appointees picked by the governor himself. They would be charged with studying the laws passed by other states and had to make recommendations by December.

The governor appointed Boston Bruins owner Charles F. Adams to the commission, and Casson was chosen to serve as vice-chairman.

The newly formed commission members held their first public hearing at the State House in October 1930. Despite all the media attention leading up to the hearing, attendance turned out to be sparse. Only ten people showed up, and only one person spoke. The lone speaker was an amateur wrestler from Cambridge, who lamented that the sport had become a racket. "I think that after all the various 'matches' we've had here, instead of Sonnenberg being the goat," he said, "it's the public."

Over the next few days, the commission continued to hold hearings elsewhere around the state. They traveled to Worcester, Springfield, Holyoke, Lawrence, Lowell, Fall River, and New Bedford, and each time they faced a room full of empty seats. No one showed up for the hearing in Lowell, with the exception of five newspaper reporters and a physician who worked for the state boxing commission.

As far as public input went, the commission didn't come away with much. Besides the man who testified at the first public hearing, only one other wrestling fan urged the commission to bring pro wrestling under strict state control.

The commission missed the original deadline for coming up with recommendations, so they returned to the Legislature and asked for more time.

On February 13, 1931, the commission released its long-awaited report. It only had one recommendation for pro wrestling that was taken directly from New York's playbook: It suggested that a law should be made requiring wrestling matches in Massachusetts to be advertised as "exhibitions."

Other than that, the commission declared that the state government could leave wrestling alone.

In its final report, the commission concluded that professional wrestling was "a theatrical exhibition of acrobatics by skilled athletes who are such masters of the art of tumbling that, on occasion, it would appear that holds and even falls have been rehearsed in advance."

But audiences loved it. The commission acknowledged that fans continued to flock to "fake" championships and thoroughly enjoyed them as a form of entertainment. The majority of the commission didn't feel that wrestling should be controlled by the state.

They stated in their final report: "This Commission does not believe it would be justified in recommending any step which would deprive the public of the enjoyment it unquestionably is now obtaining from wrestling. Just so long as the public feels it is receiving its money's worth, it will continue to support wrestling."

Casson had changed his mind about wrestling. After the final report was issued, Casson spoke openly about his belief that regulation would be detrimental to wrestling.

"To bring wrestling under honest control would kill it," Casson said. "It would remove the element of color which is now the principal attraction. The public gets a good run for its money now. Regardless of whether the contests are on the level or not, they see a good show. Wrestling without acting is a decidedly dull spectacle."

A few months later, in December 1931, Casson landed a coveted appointment in Mayor Curley's administration. His new title was the associate legislative counsel for the city of Boston, and it paid $5,000 a year—more than double the salary he earned as a legislator.

The relationships that Casson forged as a young lawmaker on the wrestling commission proved to be helpful throughout the rest of his career. By 1934, Casson was serving as the attorney for Charles F. Adams, the owner of the Boston Bruins. Casson and Adams had surely gotten to know each other better by serving on the wrestling commission together. Casson continued to serve as a legal adviser to the Bruins from the 1930s through the 1940s, and he eventually joined the Boston Garden's board of directors.

On November 21, 1931, Paul Bowser and some other wrestling promoters convened at the Bancroft Hotel in Worcester. Concerned that more legislation was in the pipeline, they decided to join forces to protect their business interests. They called themselves the Bay State Wrestling Association and said their organization was an offshoot of the American Wrestling Association. They appointed Bowser to be the chairman and went on record as opposing any political interference or legislative attempts to regulate the sport, "especially by those who know nothing at all about it."

It didn't take long for another legislator to call for governmental oversight of wrestling.

On March 30, 1933, State Senator William F. Madden of Roxbury introduced legislation to do just that. Madden was straightforward about his motivation: It was about the money. "This measure is designed to bring tax revenue into the state treasury," he said. "It makes no difference to me whether or not wrestling is a racket, but everybody who is familiar with things knows it is just that. I doubt if any wrestling match which has not been 'fixed' is held in Boston. It is a matter of business, and I see no reason why it should not be taxed, particularly in these days when we have reduced the salaries of state employees and abandoned certain departments in order to save money."

State Senator Joseph A. Langone Jr. was in his first term in the Massachusetts Legislature when he began lobbying to regulate what he called "the grunt and groan trust of Boston." Langone was a thirty-six-year-old derby-hat-wearing undertaker-turned-lawmaker from the North End, and he was not a fan of pro wrestlers.

"All they do is grunt, groan, holler, make faces, and clown around," said Langone.

And so Langone proposed a bill that would put wrestling under the supervision of the state Department of Public Safety and tack on a 10 percent tax on admission tickets to wrestling events.

By the spring of 1933, Langone grew tired of waiting for a wrestling bill to pass. He decided to inject some urgency into the situation and boldly threatened to resign if his fellow legislators didn't go with their original vote of passing the bill. Langone offered to reduce the tax to 5 percent. The lawmakers considered the measure on April 25, 1933, but they didn't do Langone any favors. Langone's legislation got nowhere. Many of his colleagues in the Senate chided him to follow through with his threat and step down.

In 1936, other bills were filed to regulate wrestling and hockey. Casson, who was now representing Adams and the Boston Bruins, opposed the bills.

The debate over the authenticity of wrestling, and whether it should be regulated, continued throughout the 1930s in states all over the country. In 1934 Henry Cauthen, a sports editor at the Charleston *News and Courier* in South Carolina, wrote that most wrestling fans knew what they were getting into. They didn't expect to see real competition. They didn't care about that. They wanted to see action. Cauthen argued that if wrestlers were really competing, "virtual murder would be committed in the ring somewhere every night."

"Fingers would be torn from men's hands, hair would be snatched from their scalps by the handful, even arms would be broken regularly and perhaps eyes would be gouged out," he wrote.

In Massachusetts, bills to regulate wrestling continued to be filed. State Representative William A. Glynn was particularly concerned about women wrestling, which he described as "an exhibition of tights and flesh." He filed a bill seeking to prohibit women from wrestling (and roller-derby matches) in 1950. He filed similar legislation in 1951, 1953, and 1954.

In 1953, State Representative Arthur W. Milne supported banning female wrestling in Massachusetts. He didn't mince his words when he spoke out against women grapplers at a public hearing.

"We outlawed cockfights many years ago, but we allow these female jackasses to get into a ring and debase themselves," Milne said. "When a cockfight is over, you have a dead chicken, but when the women grapplers get through, you have a disgrace to womanhood."

None of the bills passed.

After Milne's comments appeared in the papers, a reader wrote a letter to the editor that was published in the *Springfield Union* newspaper on February 10, 1953. The letter read, in part: "Let it be said that many of the so-called 'female jackasses' in a wrestling ring are as good, if not better than, some of the female bathers in strip-tease bathing suits rolling around the beaches of Massachusetts. Does Mr. Milne close his eyes when he goes to the beach, and would he propose a bill to forbid the sale of bathing suits in this state? Female jackasses, like male jackasses, are every-where . . . in government, on a dance floor, in automobiles, in cafes, and nightclubs. When Mr. Milne attempts to legislate morality into human lives, he is as illogical as the prohibitionists of years ago."

Ten years later—in 1963—legislation was filed in the Massachusetts state senate titled, "An Act Prohibiting Wrestling Between Women and Midgets." That bill didn't get anywhere either.

As it were, when Dropkick Murphy first started wrestling in Massachusetts, he didn't have to worry much about regulations. But as his career took off and he began to travel to wrestle in other states, he had to pay more attention. Throughout much of his career, Murphy had to keep in mind where he'd be wrestling and what rules were enforced in that state. Some states required wrestlers to be licensed. Others banned certain maneuvers.

✳ ✳ ✳

Pro wrestling made national headlines in January 1934, when politicians in New York decided they needed to shape up the sport of professional wrestling even more. The New York State Athletic Commission rewrote the rules and introduced new safety measures. Those who wrestled in the Empire State would have to wear shoes, and wrestlers could no longer toss their opponents out of the ring. There would be no "scratching, striking, gauging, butting, or strangleholds," and Murphy's trademark move—the dropkick—was also banned.

Years later, a sports columnist at the *Fitchburg Sentinel* poked fun at New York's stringent rules. Noting that the dropkick was an essential part of Murphy's repertoire, the writer mused that New York's ban on dropkicks was "possibly a deliberate scheme to keep Dr. John 'Dropkick' Murphy from ever walking off with a title . . . Murph, the Boston osteopath, who makes a habit of conking the opposition on the squash with his knee or big toe, could very well sue for 'freedom of sport' or something."

ON THE ROAD

"Dr. John 'Dropkick' Murphy, the sensational chin cracker . . ."
—*Salt Lake City Deseret News*, September 28, 1939

"The man with the cast-iron toes"
—*Los Angeles Times*, July 13, 1939

"One of the mat game's biggest box-office attractions . . ."
—*Washington Post*, April 6, 1938

A t this early stage in his career, Murphy was usually billed on wrestling cards as an outsider—a Southern playboy from Alabama or an ex-football star from the Midwest.

In between these matches, Murphy concentrated on his studies: the study of medicine and the study of wrestling. He exercised tirelessly, lifted weights, and worked out with other wrestlers, rehearsing moves and perfecting his techniques.

The more Murphy wrestled, the more polished his moves became. He gained more confidence and began to get creative, trying different maneuvers in the ring.

On Friday, April 27, 1934, Murphy caught the attention of the crowd when he came up with a new move during a match at the North Street Arena in Salem, Massachusetts.

His opponent, Lloyd Stewart, was competing barefoot, and as soon as Murphy got on top of him, he grabbed Stewart's foot and yanked his toes in opposite directions, as if he were pulling apart a wishbone. Stewart wailed in pain. The crowd cheered. Noticing how much the fans loved this, Murphy continued to employ this novel form of torture throughout the fight.

His performance was highlighted in the *Globe* the next day. The headline above the story said: "Murphy Toe Spread Amuses Everybody Except Stewart."

Dropkick Murphy returned to the North Street Arena on September 7, 1934, for what turned out to be a memorable show. Murphy's match was a preliminary bout that ended in a draw. The highlight of the show came during the battle royal at the end, which quickly spun out of control when the two remaining wrestlers, Mike Tellegen and Art Flynn, started clobbering the referee. Six men in the audience jumped into the ring to protect the referee. Police then jumped into the fray, followed by more spectators. The rioting had to be stopped. Watching this chaos unfold was City Marshal John C. Harkins, the chief of police in Salem. Afterward, he told reporters that it would be the last wrestling match held in Salem. (This ban, if it ever took effect, did not last long. Due to popular demand, wrestling quickly returned to Salem.)

To make a living as a professional wrestler, traveling was a mandatory part of the job. Many wrestlers commuted thousands of miles by car or train, going from one show to the next. Dropkick Murphy and other journeymen grapplers dreamed of wrestling at big venues in major cities. Week by week, Murphy was getting closer to achieving that goal.

In November 1934, Murphy wrestled on Thanksgiving Day in Lewiston, Maine. The following day, he was back in Salem, Massachusetts, for another show at the North Street Arena.

Murphy even wrestled on Christmas. The holiday fell on a Tuesday that year, and Murphy was part of a daylong whirlwind wrestling tour of Maine. They started with a wrestling show in the afternoon in Portland and then put on shows in Biddeford and Lewiston. The Lewiston event was only attended by about two hundred people. A sportswriter for the *Lewiston Evening Journal* snidely commented that the locals had missed a good wrestling exhibition. "Evidently Lewiston people can't leave the house on Christmas Day," he wrote.

In January 1935, Dropkick Murphy was booked to wrestle in a series of shows at the Rex Arena in Lowell. Located on the Concord River, the Rex was a former mill building that was converted into a full-fledged entertainment center complete with duckpin bowling lanes, billiard tables, and Turkish baths. For Murphy, wrestling there was a fairly easy gig, because it wasn't far from home. He'd be wrestling with many of his regular mat colleagues, including "Mad Mike" Tellegen, Fred Bruno, Steve Passas, and Jackie Nichols. There was also another familiar name on the card: Tony Siano.

A little over eight years had passed since Siano led Waltham High's football team to victory against Murphy's alma mater in Medford. After graduating in 1927, Siano went on to play football at Fordham University, where he enjoyed a spectacular collegiate career (he was an All-American and captained the team two years in a row) before turning pro and joining Boston's first NFL team, the Boston Braves, in 1932. At just five-foot-eight-inches tall and 175 pounds, Siano was one of the smallest and lightest players in the National Football League, but he performed so well that he was named captain of the Braves.

NFL players in the Great Depression earned around $140 a game, which was decent pay compared to other jobs (a typical manufacturing job paid about $17 a week in 1932). But football careers were notoriously short, and each season was only twelve weeks long, so it was important for players to find other ways of making money. Siano was no different. One of his teammates on the Braves, Jack Spellman, was a former Olympic wrestler who moonlighted on the professional wrestling circuit. After his rookie NFL season ended, Siano started appearing on wrestling cards with Spellman in 1933 and 1934.

On January 7, 1935, Dropkick Murphy and Tony Siano both wrestled on the same card at Rex Arena. Tony Siano, just a few days shy of his twenty-eighth birthday, appeared as a headliner in the main event with Al Vantres. Siano had recently wrapped up the 1934 NFL season playing for the Brooklyn Dodgers. It would also be his last. Like many other football players, Siano was shifting his focus to wrestling.

The audience watched as Siano got roughed up by Vantres, and cheered as he made his comeback. Siano wowed the crowd when he picked up Vantres and threw him out of the ring and into the first rows of seats. Vantres hurt his stomach as a result of that dramatic fall and could no longer continue, so Siano claimed the victory.

a midnight curfew was called. The convenient tie prevented another questionable champion from being crowned and saved McCloskey from presenting a belt to anyone.

Murphy was trying to wrestle as much as he could, to make money so he and his wife Marie could buy a home of their own, and he began taking on more high-profile opponents.

On October 18, 1938, Dropkick Murphy met another famous dropkicker—Jumpin' Joe Savoldi—in the ring in Newark, New Jersey. Savoldi beat Murphy in thirty-two minutes and twenty-four seconds with flying tackles and, of course, a dropkick.

Murphy would have one of the biggest matches of his career in 1939, when he went up against Jim Londos, the infamous "Golden Greek" of wrestling. They were booked as headliners for a show in Reading, Pennsylvania, a city of 110,000 that was best known for its pretzel factories and called itself the pretzel capital of the world.

In April 1939, the *Reading Eagle* reported that Murphy held the light-heavyweight championship title in New England, and he now had a chance to steal the world heavyweight title from Jim Londos.

Londos was forty-two years old and in the twilight of his career when he faced Murphy on the mat.

Bertolini started plugging Dropkick Murphy, who was twenty-six, as a young upstart who was ready to unseat the longtime champion. "Londos's days are numbered," Bertolini boasted in the *Reading Times* newspaper.

Bertolini said Murphy was versatile and just as clever as Londos.

"Murphy as champion of the world would revolutionize the sport," he said. "He has youth, plenty of color and can really wrestle."

The press coverage continued on April 18, as the *Reading Times* carried the headline: "Murphy Sees Triumph Over Champion Londos—Dropkick Artist Says Greek Idol Past His Prime."

It was a classic storyline, with the young up-and-comer aiming to take down the old veteran.

Dropkick Murphy was quoted in the newspaper saying: "Perhaps I wouldn't be talking this way about Londos three or four years ago when the Greek was in his prime, but all I can say is that if his performance against [George] Pencheff is the best he can do now, I'll throw him in less than an hour."

Whether Murphy actually uttered those words, or Bertolini wrote them himself, we'll never know (more than likely, it was the latter).

Murphy was to battle Londos on April 20 in downtown Reading. The Thursday night match was to take place at the Armory, a fortresslike venue that looked like a medieval castle. From the moment the bell rang, Londos remained in charge. Murphy managed to slip away and break out of some holds, and he put Londos in a leg lock. In the final minutes, Londos put Murphy into an arm lock. Murphy tried some flying tackles, but Londos caught him in midair and knocked him down to the mat. Londos fought to control the young grappler, and Murphy wriggled free three times. But then Londos hoisted Murphy's whole body up over his shoulders and began spinning around. He then slammed Murphy down on the canvas and pinned him for the win. They had wrestled for nearly thirty-two minutes. Londos claimed the victory and held onto his heavyweight title, as was expected.

Murphy met Londos again on May 10, 1939. This time they wrestled at the Madrid Palestra. Before the match, Murphy bragged about his endurance in the pages of the Harrisburg newspaper, *Evening News*, promising that he would outlast Londos. But alas, that bold prediction would not come to pass. According to newspaper accounts of the match, Murphy at one point fell and landed on his stomach. Londos climbed on top of him and put one boot on Murphy's back, then grabbed both of Murphy's arms and pulled them back. Murphy grimaced and scowled in pain as his shoulder blades were squeezed together. Londos held him in this prone position—known as a "surfboard hold"—until Murphy conceded defeat. Londos won the match and once again retained his role as champion.

Murphy continued to travel through the summer of 1939. In June, he wrestled in Washington, D.C., then he headed to the West Coast and wrestled at the Coliseum Athletic Club in San Diego. In September, Murphy journeyed to Salt Lake City to wrestle in the season opener at McCullough's Arena, which was known as "Utah's little Madison Square Garden."

Les Goates, a sports columnist for the *Deseret News* in Utah, was impressed by Murphy's athleticism and marveled at the way he unleashed his dropkick from a prone position. He made it look so easy. "Murphy uncoils like a great cobra, almost effortless," Goates wrote in his column on September 16, 1939. He "comes end-over-end, and those feet [are] astonishingly accurate."

January 1940 proved to be a busy time for Johnny Murphy. He continued to wrestle locally in Boston and Lowell. He also took on Karol Krauser in New York City, Jersey City, New Jersey, and Bridgeport, Connecticut. (Krauser was known for his muscular physique and actually served as the artist's model for the first animated cartoon version of Superman.)

Meanwhile, Pennsylvanian promoter Bert Bertolini got a head start with publicizing Dropkick Murphy's upcoming match in his territory: a one-fall match at the Reading Armory on February 6, 1940, against Rene LaBelle, a wrestler known as the "French Mat Wizard."

LaBelle had a slightly bulbous nose and full lips. Sometimes he shaved his dark hair off so he was bald.

Once again, Bertolini was trying to drum up publicity for the bout by getting as much ink as he could in the local newspapers. On January 30, 1940, the *Reading Eagle* reported that Bertolini had been aggressively recruiting Murphy for this match. The newspaper also chronicled the escalating hostility between the two feuding grapplers. Bertolini continued to stoke this melodrama to boost anticipation for the upcoming bout. The *Reading Eagle* started calling Murphy "The Blond Bomber" and boasted that he was a top heavyweight contender who'd gone undefeated for two years while competing in New England.

"Murphy's dropkicks are the best in the business and his acrobatic stunts keeps his rivals up in the air as well as the audience," declared a story in the paper on February 4, 1940. "The Boston Irishman can travel at top speed for two hours if necessary. He is a tireless performer and lives and talks wrestling."

LaBelle countered those statements with confidence. "I want to be the only wrestler ever to hold four different world titles, and Dropkick

Murphy or no one else is going to change my mind," LaBelle (supposedly) told a reporter in a long-distance phone call from Boston with promoter Bertolini.

LaBelle was a twenty-eight-year-old underdog in the one-fall match against Murphy.

Murphy matched him hold for hold and almost won until LaBelle socked him with a flying dropkick and pinned him. To everyone's surprise, LaBelle won.

After that loss, Murphy quickly challenged LaBelle to a rematch, and, naturally, LaBelle accepted.

Bertolini needed to infuse more drama into the ongoing feud and wanted Dropkick to up the ante. On February 25, 1940, the *Reading Eagle* reported that Murphy had been working out at a gymnasium in Philadelphia, getting ready for his rematch with LaBelle. It was two days away. "If I can't beat that Frenchman I'll retire," said Murphy. "I'm really surprised that he agreed to wrestle me again. He was offered three times as much money to meet me in Boston but refused."

"Murphy to Quit Wrestling if He Loses to LaBelle" proclaimed the *Eagle* headline.

On Tuesday, February 27, 1940, Murphy and LaBelle met once again at the Reading Armory. They each exchanged dropkicks to each other's stomachs. At one point, one of Murphy kicks went astray and knocked out a ring post. He had planned to bounce off the taut ropes but the post gave way, and Murphy looked shocked when the ropes sagged. There was a brief delay while the ring was fixed. The battle went on for forty-eight minutes and thirty-two seconds, until the state curfew law of 11:30 p.m. went into effect, and the bout was declared a draw. The two combatants didn't want to stop though. Murphy and LaBelle traded words and punches and had to be physically separated after the match ended.

Dropkick Murphy's vow to quit wrestling wasn't just another contrived storyline to get people in the door to attend that particular match. This time, there was some truth to it. Murphy was about to enter the next stage of his life.

7

HEALTH FARMER

*The body does not wear out; people abuse it and
wear it out. You can always rebuild when you go about
the task intelligently.*
—William Muldoon

I n May 1940, Dropkick Murphy's wife Marie gave birth to their second child. The baby was a boy, and they named him David. When David turned eleven days old, the couple bid goodbye to Murphy's mother and left the house on St. Mary Street. They drove twenty miles to their new home in the rural suburb of Acton.

Acton was more than twice the geographical size of Medford but had only a fraction of the people. It was an old community with a long memory. Originally part of Concord, it was incorporated as an independent town in 1735. Actonians were proud of the town's history and the role their forefathers played in the American Revolution.

Of the 2,700 people who lived in Acton in 1940, the population was predominantly white. The more established families were descendants of Revolutionary War veterans. Newer arrivals included immigrants from Nova Scotia, Italy, and Norway.

While Murphy's hometown of Medford was densely populated, Acton was not. It had a rustic, rural character. Instead of factories and stores, there were farms and apple orchards. With twenty square miles of gentle hills, woods, and farmland, the air felt different out there—fresh, clean, crisp. It was nothing like the thick, fume-laden layer of smog that often blanketed the cities that Murphy frequented on the wrestling circuit.

There weren't many automobiles in Acton, but traffic was increasing because so many people were traveling through the town to get to Fort Devens, where Army draftees from all over New England came to train before being deployed for combat in World War II. When Murphy moved to Acton, the town had just hired a part-time police officer to direct traffic, and additional speed-limit signs were being installed.

Meanwhile, the townspeople were desperately clinging onto traditional values. Local voters had narrowly defeated proposals to allow beer, wine, and liquor to be sold in town. The school system remained small, with five hundred students total and forty in the graduating class.

It was in Acton that Murphy was introduced to Bellows Farm, which would become the biggest purchase of his life. The farmland spanned more than eighty acres in the northern part of town. As Murphy walked around the property, he probably looked around, taking it all in. It had a completely different feel than Boston, Medford, and other cities where he wrestled. Out there, the landscape was dominated by seemingly endless expanses of green trees, open fields, rolling hills, and apple orchards. The air was filled with a peace and quiet that Murphy would grow to appreciate. Perhaps he envisioned himself retiring there.

Bellows Farm was named such because a previous owner, Ebenezer Davis, once had a shop there where he manufactured bellows, devices used to blow air onto fires. It later became a dairy farm.

In 1934 the farm closed, and the cattle, horses, and farm equipment were put up for sale at a public auction. In March 1940, the farm was advertised as being available for rent. It was around that time that Murphy bought the property.

In May, soon after David was born, Murphy and his wife and children moved into the big house at Bellows Farm. Located at 40 Davis Road, the distinguished colonial home had white clapboards and green shutters, a thick chimney protruding from the roof, and a farmer's porch in front. It contained a dozen rooms, which would provide more than enough space for the Murphys and their two little boys.

John and Marie immediately put their medical expertise to work. He had a degree in osteopathic medicine, she was a registered nurse, and together they operated a convalescent home at Bellows Farm. But not for long. Big changes were coming.

Dropkick Murphy had always been fascinated by the concept of a "health farm," especially one in New York that was operated by William J. Brown.

Brown was thirty-eight years older than Murphy and was a legend in the world of boxing. Born in County Cork, Ireland, in 1874, he came to the United States with his widowed mother and made a name for himself wrestling at the turn of the century. He landed a job as an instructor at a gymnasium in New York and eventually opened a gym of his own, where he trained countless police officers and firefighters and got them into shape. He also started his own fight club (at 115 West 23rd Street in New York City) and did quite well hosting boxing matches.

At the time, boxing was only allowed among members of the same athletic club, and the enterprising Irishman took advantage of that loophole by having his contenders join his club before entering the ring. In 1909, Brown took his earnings and bought a farm overlooking the Hudson River in Garrison, New York—across the from the U.S. Military Academy at West Point—and turned it into a training center for men of all ages and occupations. He called it "Bill Brown's Physical Training Farm," and people who stayed there could go on walks, go jogging, drink carrot juice, take in plenty of fresh air, and relax in steam baths and saunas to sweat out toxins.

His thirty-five-bed facility was located an hour north of Manhattan, and his clientele, whom he referred to as "guests," included bankers, judges, members of the Brooklyn Dodgers, and luminaries such as Congressman Hamilton Fish, author Sinclair Lewis, filmmaker John Ford, boxer Joe Louis, and Hollywood mogul Winfield R. Sheehan (who produced films starring Ginger Rogers and Shirley Temple). A writer from the *New Yorker* described Brown's 380-acre oasis as "an unexcelled retreat from fashion and females," a place where businessmen could escape the pressures of the city and put aside their day-to-day worries to focus on their physical health and well-being.

Every morning guests would be woken up at dawn and start the day exercising with dumbbells in the gym. After breakfast Brown led his guests on a long hike that ended with a quarter-mile climb up Salvation Hill, which the guests named "Damnation Hill." That was followed by a massage and then lunch, and then sports in the afternoon. Brown offered horseback riding, tennis, squash, handball, swimming, and a limited amount of golf, a sport of which Brown was not particularly fond. ("Golf was invented for expectant mothers," he once said.) Brown recommended that guests stay for at least two weeks to see results; many stayed four to six weeks.

Brown despised alcohol and cigarettes, and perhaps not surprisingly, his farm became, by default, a place where prominent men could take a temporary break from not only their careers but from drinking as well. Brown didn't enjoy that part of it, though. One time a woman brought her inebriated husband to him, and Brown refused to take him in. "Get him out of here," he told her. "When you quit drinking yourself, bring your husband back here and maybe I'll help him."

Brown's resort was well-known, and to Murphy it seemed like a dream job. But Brown wasn't the first athlete to open such a place. Martin Flaherty, a professional boxer from Lowell, opened a health farm in Tewksbury, Massachusetts, in 1904. Known as the Wamesit Health Farm, it was a place where boxers could work out and members of the public could participate in archery, golf, horseback riding, and other activities. Flaherty welcomed "nervous cases" as well as people who wanted to lose weight and "retain youth at middle age." Pro boxers such as Dick "Honeyboy" Finnegan and Jack Sharkey trained there in the 1920s.

Another well-known health farm in Massachusetts was operated by Dr. John W. Bowler, a professor of physical education and hygiene at Dartmouth College. Bowler's health farm was located in Marlborough in the 1910s and 1920s, and he specialized in treating men who were run down "from overwork, overstrain, or other causes" and people suffering from obesity, heart trouble, chronic indigestion, constipation, and a condition known as "neurasthenia," an outdated medical term that was used to describe someone who was drained of their nervous energy. Symptoms included indigestion, fatigue, muscle pain, impotence, infertility, depression, and irrationality. (While it is no longer diagnosed today, it's interesting to note that some of the symptoms are similar to what is now called chronic fatigue syndrome.)

The health farm concept can be traced back even earlier thanks to the efforts of William Muldoon, an accomplished wrestler who became a leader in promoting physical fitness in the late nineteenth century. One of Muldoon's famous clients was bare-knuckle boxing champ John L. Sullivan. In 1889, Muldoon hosted Sullivan at his home in Belfast, New York, and helped him dry out and prepare for his next bout. Muldoon led Sullivan on long runs, refused to let him smoke, and limited Sullivan's alcohol intake to less than a glass of ale a day.

Sullivan hated it.

Journalist Nellie Bly visited Muldoon's home while Sullivan was training and wrote an article about it for the *New York World* newspaper. Muldoon told Bly that he wasn't looking to become wealthy by turning his home into Sullivan's training facility. "I don't make any money by this," he said, "but I was anxious to see Mr. Sullivan do justice to himself in this coming fight. It was a case of a fallen giant, so I thought to get him away from all bad influences and to get him in good trim. This is the healthiest place in the country, and one of the [most] difficult to reach—two desirable things."

Bly asked Sullivan how he liked training thus far.

"It's the worst thing going," Sullivan said. "A fellow would rather fight twelve dozen times than train once, but it's got to be done."

Muldoon continued to provide personal fitness training services to men of means at his estate known as "The Maples" in White Plains, New York. In the summer of 1895, a newspaper reporter came out to The Maples for a tour of the facilities, which included a gymnasium and horse stables. "This is where I repair the human machinery of the depressed, the exhausted, the overworked," Muldoon said. He went on to establish Olympia, a "hygienic institute" in Purchase, New York, in 1900 and served as a personal fitness trainer to top bankers, lawyers, and politicians.

Muldoon was a tough character with plenty of stamina; so much so, in fact, that he was once described as having "more energy than a ton of benzedrine inhalers."

Muldoon always referred to Olympia as a hygienic institute, not as a health farm. In his mind, a health farm was for drunks. "I have no faith in alcohol," Muldoon once said. "Nothing else destroys the muscular tissues as readily as does alcohol." And although Muldoon was once quoted as saying "I don't take alcoholics," some of them did make their way to his institute. Muldoon tolerated them at Olympia, so long as they gave up alcohol completely and adhered to his strict set of rules.

Dropkick Murphy aimed to do something similar at Bellows Farm. But unlike Bill Brown and William Muldoon, who merely tolerated alcoholics, Dropkick Murphy embraced them. He wanted to help as many drinkers as he could.

Murphy may have also been inspired by Valleyhead Hospital, a private sanitarium located in the neighboring town of Carlisle, Massachusetts. It was started by a psychiatrist named Dr. Lawrence K. Lunt on a piece of farmland known as Wilson Stock Farm. It was a short drive from Bellows Farm.

Valleyhead first opened its doors to patients in 1929. It catered to patients of means who suffered from depression, schizophrenia, and alcohol and drug addiction. The hospital featured squash and tennis courts, a swimming pool, a bowling alley, a shooting gallery, and a large room where badminton could be played. Jackie Kennedy and Sylvia Plath were among many well-known patients who sought treatment there.

The idea of bringing alcoholics to Bellows Farm—the same place where they were raising their children—was probably the topic of many lively discussions between Murphy and his wife, Marie. No one knows for sure how long they debated and considered the idea, but at some point the Murphys came to a decision: They would expand their reach to a wider clientele by offering services for people trying to dry out from booze.

Years later, when he was asked the question of how he got into the business of drying out alcoholics, Murphy liked to say: "Chance. Sheer unadulterated chance."

Murphy would tell the story of how it all began and recount a story from his days in the ring. It was soon after they moved to Acton, and Murphy had found himself caring for three alcoholics.

"I was asked if I could straighten out three alkies," he said. "You know, put them on the farm, shovel good food into them, and let them breathe fresh air."

Murphy told his wife about his mission. The guys are great, but they didn't eat. "They just sit around and shake," said Murphy.

One night Murphy was scheduled to wrestle at Valley Arena in Holyoke, and he brought the three guys along. They were stone-cold sober and looking forward to watching Murphy perform in the ring. They traveled ninety miles west to Holyoke, an industrial city in western Massachusetts known for its paper mills. The Valley Arena was located on Bridge Street in an old gas-works building. The 1884 "gas house" was converted into a sporting venue in 1926 and hosted boxing matches, wrestling events, and concerts by big-time orchestras led by Benny Goodman and Glenn Miller. Joe Louis once refereed a wrestling match at Valley Arena, and many great boxers fought there, including Willie Pep, Tony DeMarco, and Rocky Marciano, who made his pro debut there on St. Patrick's Day in 1947.

That night Murphy's opponent was "Wild Bull" Curry, a former police officer from Hartford, Connecticut, and they called him "wild" for a reason. Curry was about the same age as Murphy—he was born in 1913—and was a veteran of the pro wrestling circuits. He was of Lebanese descent, and his head and chest were covered with a thick mat of black frizzy hair. His bushy, arched eyebrows formed into one magnificently thick unibrow that traversed much of his lower forehead. The hirsute, raven-eyed grappler was a pioneer in hardcore over-the-top moves and a well-known villain who knew exactly how to drive crowds into a frenzy. He would often scowl and contort his mouth into a maniacal facial expression. Curry was a fearless stuntman who loved to stir up trouble. When he'd get thrown out of the ring, he'd often land right on top of beer vendors, and even into the laps of unsuspecting athletic commissioners.

On the night of the match, Murphy sat his three pals in one of the back rows and then went down to the locker room to get ready. Eventually Murphy and Curry emerged from the dressing room and entered the ring. With the sound of the bell, the match started, just as it always did, but this time was different because Murphy was responsible for three recovering drunks in the audience. But he wasn't worried. Not one bit.

"I didn't know anything about booze and the way it pulls a guy," recalled Murphy, many years later.

"They were cold sober," he said, "and soon Bull and I were slamming each other all over the ring. Then we heard a terrible commotion."

Murphy usually didn't look beyond the ropes. But this time, when he glanced up into the seats, he couldn't believe what he saw.

"We looked up and there were my three friends, yelling and weaving and swaying—bombed to the eyeballs," he said.

The transformation of his three buddies from regular, mild-mannered fans to loud, obnoxious drunks weighed heavy on Murphy's mind. Murphy found his new calling.

"I whisked them back to Acton, and I guess I was hooked," Murphy said.

Murphy said he called Paul Bowser and told him he was done with wrestling professionally. From now on his vision would be fixated on something much bigger, something that was beyond the ring. After fighting the same burly opponents for years and years, Murphy now faced a completely new challenge: alcoholics.

"I guess every family has a booze problem—somewhere there's an aunt, uncle, a sister or brother, or even a mother or father, someone, somewhere," Dropkick once said. "[It's] the only disease you can get arrested for."

Murphy had realistic expectations: Never did he think he could magically rehabilitate or cure alcoholics. But he could help them get sober for a little while, at least.

His wrestling career had taken him to Boston Arena, Madison Square Garden, the New York Coliseum, and to New Jersey, Connecticut, Rhode Island, Maine, Quebec, California, Pennsylvania, Utah, and Washington, D.C.

But now his focus would be in Acton.

Just like the bellows that breathed life back into flames, Dropkick Murphy brought life back to alcoholics, helping them become whole again, Murphy aimed to help them reignite their internal spark by keeping them off booze. Even if it was only temporary—to him, it was a worthwhile thing.

Murphy had seen what alcohol did to people in the wrestling world.

It was no secret that Julius Woronick, the wrestler better known as the "Great Mephisto," had a serious drinking problem. He'd been charged with drunk driving more than once and had been arrested for assaulting his mother in 1931. Newspapers reported that he beat up his mother because she didn't have his breakfast ready when he woke up at one o'clock in the afternoon. He was arrested for a similar offense in 1962, after he allegedly pulled his mother out of bed, hit her in the head, and stomped on her. His mother ended up in the hospital. When authorities questioned him about his violent outburst, he told them he had no memory of the incident.

Woronick wasn't the only wrestler to get into trouble with the law. On the night of July 18, 1932, Gus Sonnenberg had a wrestling match in Haverhill, a city thirty-five miles north of Boston. After the show was over, he went out with the promoter, Patrick J. Lucy, and the referee, Leon Burbank, to a local Elks club, where they stayed until the early morning. When they finally left the club around 3:30 a.m., Sonnenberg got in his roadster and started following Burbank's car into North Andover. Suddenly, the bright glow of headlights took over his windshield, followed by a terrible crash. That was the last thing Sonnenberg said he remembered until he woke up slumped over his broken steering wheel. Blood dripped from his finger, and he felt pain in his chest. He heard the voice of Burbank, the referee, saying, "How are you, boy?"

"I'm hurt," said Sonnenberg.

The crash had occurred near the intersection of Osgood Street and Great Pond Road in North Andover. It was a head-on collision. The driver of the other car—a Lawrence police officer named Richard L. Morrissey—was seriously injured, his face badly cut. Both men were taken to Lawrence General Hospital and were placed in adjoining beds. Morrissey's brother arrived at the hospital room and asked Sonnenberg what had happened. Sonnenberg didn't provide many details, just saying that neither saw each other coming and it was "all a blank."

Sonnenberg spent the day in the hospital and was discharged later that evening. He then went to his wife's parents' house at 71 Payson Road in Belmont to recuperate from his injuries. He was slated to wrestle the following night (July 21) at Braves Field before a crowd of twenty-five thousand, including Mayor Curley. But Sonnenberg stayed out of the ring, and Paul Bowser found a substitute to take his place.

Morrissey, however, wasn't as lucky. He remained in the hospital on the danger list. On July 22, he succumbed to his injuries and died.

Early in the morning on July 30, Sonnenberg's father-in-law, John Elliott, heard someone at his door. When he answered, he found himself facing an entourage of police. The group included the North Andover police chief, two inspectors from the Lawrence Police Department, and a Belmont patrol officer. They had a warrant out for Sonnenberg's arrest. He was being charged with manslaughter, operating to endanger, and operating under the influence of liquor. Sonnenberg was sleeping when the police arrived and was cooperative once he woke up. He left with the police and was driven to the Belmont police station, where he was officially booked.

Sonnenberg's father got into his own car and drove into Boston to pick up Paul Bowser.

Sonnenberg limped as he walked into Lawrence District Court that morning for his arraignment. He appeared before Judge Frederic N. Chandler and pleaded not guilty to all charges. He was ordered held on $2,000 bail, which Bowser posted on his behalf.

The news of Sonnenberg's arrest made headlines across the country. A major radio network asked to broadcast Sonnenberg's trial. Judge Chandler said no.

"Fame or lack of fame makes no difference before me," Chandler said. "Sonnenberg will be tried according to the evidence before me and will be so judged and treated. As for the need of broadcast to give information to the public, the people will get all the information they want from the newspapers."

Sonnenberg's trial took place on August 2, 1932. The prosecution called eleven witnesses to testify. One was an ambulance driver who said he'd smelled alcohol on Sonnenberg's breath on the night of the accident. Another was a Lawrence police officer who testified that one of the nurses at the hospital told him that she'd smelled beer on Sonnenberg's breath on the night of the accident. The officer also testified that the nurse remarked that Sonnenberg was "stewed" in the operating room, and that a doctor overheard her comment. But when the nurse was called to the stand, she balked. When the prosecutor asked if she noticed any signs that Sonnenberg had been drinking, she replied: "There was a stale odor to his breath."

"Was there any smell of liquor?" the prosecutor asked.

The nurse hesitated. "No," she said.

"Was there any smell of beer?"

"I don't know."

"Did you say in the operating room, 'He's stewed'?"

The nurse said she couldn't recall.

When the doctor took the stand, the prosecutor asked if he overheard anyone talking about Sonnenberg being "stewed." The doctor said no. He said he overheard someone say, "I wonder if he is under the influence of liquor."

The defense did not call any witnesses, and the judge moved quickly on the case. On August 2, Sonnenberg was found not guilty of manslaughter, but he was convicted for driving under the influence of liquor and driving to endanger.

After the verdict, Judge Chandler called before him the doctor and two nurses from Lawrence General Hospital who had been called as witnesses. He was clearly not happy with their testimony. "I am satisfied that there has been concealment and perjury in your testimony," Chandler said, "and I have every right to cite you for contempt and deal with you accordingly. But I am taking into consideration the fact that two of you are women and the other is a young man just starting his professional career."

The judge said it wasn't the first time that witnesses from their hospital had withheld evidence in a case, and he ordered them to go back to their superiors at the hospital and tell them it had to stop.

Chandler sentenced Sonnenberg to three months in jail and fined him $100.

Sonnenberg promptly appealed. The case went up to superior court, and Sonnenberg was tried again in February 1933. During that trial a bartender from the Elks club testified that he had seen Sonnenberg drink beer at the club and noticed that he was unsteady on his feet at times as the night wore on. But when Sonnenberg took the stand, he denied drinking anything more than ginger ale. Several other witnesses testified on his behalf, including Paul Bowser.

The jury was swayed by Sonnenberg's testimony and that of his friends.

On March 2, 1933, in Essex County Superior Court, Sonnenberg was found not guilty of driving to endanger and operating under the influence. After the foreman read the verdict in the crowded courtroom, one of Sonnenberg's lawyers slapped him on the back. Sonnenberg smiled and began shaking the hands of each juror.

A few years later, Paul Bowser found himself embroiled in another drinking-and-driving case.

It happened on March 11, 1936. Around six o'clock that evening, Bowser's wife, Cora, was driving through Newton, a suburb of Boston. At the corner of Centre and Walnut streets, she allegedly struck a twenty-seven-year-old pedestrian, knocking him over and injuring his arm.

But Cora never stopped. When a police officer who witnessed the collision attempted to stop her, she apparently kept on going and sped away. An alert went out to local police stations. Cora was eventually pulled over by police in the neighboring town of Wellesley, where she was arrested. Officers who questioned her at the station said her "speech was thick." They charged her with drunkenness, operating under the influence of liquor, leaving the scene of an accident, and driving without having her license in her possession.

It was an embarrassing episode for both Cora and her husband, as the incident was reported in the newspapers. Cora was already well-known from her own professional wrestling career. Once upon a time, she was a headline act at the Old Howard burlesque theater in Boston's Scollay Square, where she challenged everyone and took all comers. At the height of her fame, she was considered to be the best female wrestler in the world.

On March 12 she appeared in Newton District Court and pleaded not guilty to drunk-driving and other charges. She was released on $500 bail. Six days later she returned to court and was found guilty of two of the charges—operating under the influence and leaving the scene of the accident—and was fined $200.

The treatment of alcoholism had undergone many changes in America, and Murphy decided to get into the business at an opportune time. There weren't enough sober houses to meet demand. Alcoholics seeking treatment had few options to choose from—they could either check themselves into a hospital, or they could seek out a private sanitarium where they could dry out. Bellows Farm fell into the latter category, which in street terms was known as a "spin-dry" or "jitter joint."

According to William L. White, author of *Slaying the Dragon: The History of Addiction Treatment and Recovery in America*, there were many such farms/sanitaria that operated from the late nineteenth through the mid-twentieth century. White said most of these institutions closed during the Prohibition years, or during the 1960s and 1970s, when professionalized addiction treatment became more available because of increased state and federal funding.

By the time Prohibition went into effect in 1920, the only public inebriate hospital in Massachusetts had closed its doors. The Massachusetts Hospital for Dipsomaniacs and Inebriates had opened in Foxborough in 1893 and was believed to be the first publicly funded treatment facility of its kind in the country. The law allowed for men to be committed for up to two years. If they followed the rules and attended all the required classes, they could take a leave of absence from the hospital after six months. Although Foxborough was initially hailed as a pioneering institution that was full of promise and success stories, it did not last.

State officials later decided to change the Foxborough facility into a mental hospital for the insane, and in 1914 the substance-use patients were relocated to Norfolk State Hospital. A few years later, during World War I, the federal government took over the Norfolk campus and used it as a military hospital. After the war, the state resumed control of the property and turned it into a hospital for cancer patients.

With the loss of Norfolk State Hospital, alcoholics and drug addicts were either sent to the state farm in Bridgewater, which was run by the Department of Correction, or they were dropped off at Boston City Hospital.

In the years to come, the numbers of alcoholics coming to Boston City Hospital grew exponentially. Between 1915 and 1929, the number of cases increased from 487 to 2,052—and those were only the most serious cases, where the police felt that the person required treatment. By 1936, doctors declared alcoholism to be the "greatest and most expensive problem" at the hospital.

Almost a decade later, the state of Massachusetts was still grappling with the problem of what to do with alcoholics. In 1945—a quarter of a century after the Norfolk State Hospital had closed its doors and a dozen years after the repeal of Prohibition—a special commission appointed by the Legislature to investigate the "problem of drunkenness" in Massachusetts reported some disappointing findings:

It may seem ironical that at the conclusion of this study our thoughts and recommendations finally have become crystallized along the same general trends which repeatedly have been called to the attention of the General Court during the past thirty-five years through the media of special messages or special reports. . . . We see no other alternative to curb drunkenness in its broadest aspects on a state-wide basis, except those measures that the State has tried and failed in.

In December 1946 Mayor James Michael Curley posed a question to Maxwell Grossman, the state commissioner of penal institutions: "How many drunks is the city supporting at Deer Island and the Charles Street Jail?"

"Eighty percent of all the prisoners are there because they're drunks," Grossman replied.

Curley suggested opening a public hospital for alcoholics on Long Island (located in the Boston Harbor) or the Charles Street Jail in Boston. To finance such a project, he recommended raising the fees for liquor licenses.

While government officials debated about what should be done, people struggling with substance-use issues continued to seek help on their own, and not always with the best results. Countless alcoholics—as well as their loved ones—desperately put their faith into quack cures. Several for-profit enterprises sprung up in the late nineteenth century to serve this clientele. One of the most popular franchises was founded by Dr. Leslie E. Keeley, a doctor in Illinois who claimed to have invented a medicine to treat alcoholism and morphine addiction. "Drunkenness is a disease and I can cure it," was his personal slogan. He marketed his proprietary remedy as the "Keeley Cure" and claimed that it contained "bichloride of gold." Those undergoing treatment would drink his special tonic and receive four hypodermic shots daily. (Medical experts tried to identify the secret ingredients in Keeley's formula. According to one medical journal, there was no gold in the tonic, but ironically enough, it did contain 27.55 percent alcohol.)

Branches of his Keeley Institute popped up all over the country, and several outposts operated in Massachusetts (at one point there were Keeley Institute locations in Lexington, Haverhill, Springfield, North Adams, and Worcester). There was even an auxiliary organization for members' wives, mothers, sisters, and daughters.

Another franchise that made big promises was the Neal Institute, which started in Iowa in 1892 and pledged to cure anyone's "drink habit" in just three days. It grew into a national franchise with more than sixty locations across the country. When the Boston location opened at 304 Newbury Street in 1910, the Neal Institute assured that its "Three-Day Drink Habit Cure" was "purely vegetable" and boasted of "freeing victims from the bondage of desire, craving, and appetite for drink." The Neal Institute's quick cure continued to be advertised through the 1940s.

Mail-order ads for miracle pills appeared in newspapers in the late 1930s and early 1940s. One Boston-based druggist, G. S. Cheney Co. at 15 Union Street, marketed bottles of vitamin B1 tablets as a remedy for chronic alcoholism and other ailments.

Public health officials recognized that something had to change. In 1937, Dr. Henry D. Chadwick, the state commissioner of public health, argued that alcoholics needed treatment and medical care in a proper setting. "Chronic drunks are now sent to the Bridgewater State Farm . . . left there for a short period to sober up, and then let go."

Chadwick felt that chronic alcoholism was a disease, not a crime. He recommended that the state provide health facilities "where victims of alcohol may be sent by the courts for treatment in the same manner as mental patients are referred."

Boston Municipal Court Judge Elijah Adlow echoed those sentiments when he spoke at a banquet in downtown Boston in 1938. He told the crowd that Boston had nineteen thousand drunkenness cases a year and that society's present approach of dealing with alcoholics was "one that is not sane."

"The vicious cycle repeats itself—arrest, court, jail or state farm, over and over again," he said.

One of the most bizarre proposals for dealing with alcoholics in Massachusetts came from the mayor of Woburn, a city just outside of Boston. "Woburn is going to solve its problem of drunkenness with my lion's cage," proclaimed Woburn Mayor William E. Kane in 1938. Kane's bold plan involved putting drunks into a large portable cage attached to a police cruiser, so they could be wheeled through the streets and subjected to public humiliation while they sobered up. Kane even traveled to Benson's animal farm in Nashua, New Hampshire, to check out the cages there for inspiration.

The mayor really did get a cage, as he promised. When his horse-drawn jail made its debut and rolled through the streets of Woburn on March 23, 1938, Kane marched proudly beside it.

"Well, I guess I'm not bluffing now," he said.

The cage remained empty, but Kane used it as a billboard, posting signs that read "WARNING! DRUNKEN DRIVERS BEWARE," and had a horse named Mary pull it all the way into Boston to show off his cage in front of the State House.

Kane's publicity stunt illustrated society's uncertainty of how to deal with problem drinkers and the lack of resources that were available at the time. The dearth of treatment options gave rise to private sanitaria that catered to affluent customers who were able to pay for detox services.

✿ ✿ ✿

Two years after Prohibition ended, a new option for alcoholics emerged: Alcoholics Anonymous. The first A.A. meetings were held in Ohio, and the program began to spread to other states. As more people began to learn about it, membership increased. The demand was surely there, and A.A. filled the need.

A pivotal moment for the public's awareness and perception of alcoholism occurred in the spring of 1940, thanks to a professional baseball player named Ralston B. Hemsley. "Rollicking Rollie" was an all-star catcher who drank heavily and bounced from team to team in the major leagues because he got into so much trouble. From smashing a dresser drawer over a photographer's head to throwing punches at policemen, Rollie did it all, with the rambunctious bravado of a pro athlete with nothing to lose. Legend goes that one time he slid into a base and hobbled off the field in pain because a bottle of booze smashed inside his pants pocket, leaving shards of glass in his leg.

Another incident occurred in 1939, while Hemsley was riding with the team on a train. Sometime during the night, Hemsley and a *New York Times* correspondent started fooling around with a trumpet. Their antics woke up the team's travel secretary, Lewis Mumaw, who poked his head out of his berth and told them to keep it down. "Oh, you've got a beef," said Hemsley. "We'll fix that." Hemsley, ever the jokester, began tossing lit matches into Mumaw's berth. Then he yelled, "We'll have to put out the fire!" and started pouring water all over Mumaw.

As a result of those drunken exploits, Hemsley ended up getting suspended. When a reporter asked the team's manager, Oscar Vitt, how he found out about Hemsley's behavior, he was quick to reply.

"How did I learn?" said Vitt. "Why the guy was right in my berth from midnight to four o'clock this morning. Half the time he was abusive and half the time he was crying."

But the story Hemsley became most famous for happened on April 16, 1940. It was opening day for the Cleveland Indians, and the team had traveled to Chicago to play the White Sox. Hemsley picked up the telephone and called each of the sportswriters who were there to cover the game. "Meet me on the hotel mezzanine." The press did as he instructed, each waiting, wondering, speculating about what kind of bombshell the old pro might drop—that is, if he even showed up.

Helmsley did show up. And what he told the press shocked not only them, but everyone else in America who would later read the words in newspapers across the country.

"It's been just a year now since the most wonderful thing in the world happened to me, so I feel safe in telling you boys about it. You know I didn't have a drink all last season. Well, Alcoholics Anonymous did that for me. I'd like to give credit to this great organization and you'll do me a favor by writing a story about A.A."

Hemsley would later describe how he got involved with A.A. "I had tried everything else, and these fellows at least weren't giving me theories. They themselves had conquered the same weakness which was ruining me. They told me about dozens of other fellows—some of them prominent citizens—who had the same experience. I could see they were sincere—and I was desperate. I went with them. It was the most fortunate decision of my life."

The star catcher's confession shed light on a problem that had been kept hush-hush for generations, and newspapers across the country ran stories about Hemsley's experience with this new, life-changing organization known as Alcoholics Anonymous. The publicity raised the profile of A.A., which brought in more members, and the number of A.A. groups continued to grow.

A man by the name of Paddy K. started the first known A.A. group in Boston in 1940. That was the same year Dropkick Murphy moved to Acton and took over Bellows Farm. It wouldn't be long before he started hosting A.A. meetings out there as well.

In June 1945 Murphy welcomed representatives from the Boston and Cleveland A.A. chapters to Bellows Farm so his patients could learn more about the organization. About thirty people listened with interest as they explained how A.A. worked.

The *Acton Beacon* newspaper ran a story about the meeting the following week and reported that A.A. "has mushroomed into a society with groups in all the larger cities and many towns," including Boston, where a local chapter met every Wednesday night at 306 Newbury Street, and the public was invited to attend.

"As every member is a reformed alcoholic, each appreciates the struggle ahead for the prospective member, and each helps unstintingly until the time arrives when the new member may be trusted alone," the article stated. "The friendly unselfishness of these reformed alcoholics is primarily responsible for the great growth of the organization."

Bellows Farm eventually launched its own A.A. group and started holding weekly meetings at the farm on Wednesday nights. Dropkick Murphy held A.A. in high regard.

"I think A.A. is great," said Murphy. "They know what they're doing."

In addition to the occasional articles published by the local paper, Murphy placed advertisements in newspapers to publicize his new venture. One of his first ads ran in the *Boston Herald* on December 8, 1940. It appeared in the classified ads under the "Health and Rest Homes" category:

TIRED?
BELLOWS FARM, 1760 Colonial homestead, restful atmosphere,
business and professional people; one hour from Boston. Tel. Acton
496, ring 22.

Murphy ran similar ads in the *Lowell Sun* and the *Boston Globe*.

Later, Murphy decided to update the ad and extend his reach to a wider audience. On July 5, 1942, he took out a classified ad in the *New York Times* and used words that hinted that Bellows Farm was also a detox facility:

BELLOWS FARM.
Tired—need a rest? An 80-acre farm ideal for nervous, tired people;
operated by young people; registered nurse; 25 miles from Boston;
train service; $25 per week. Acton, Mass. Phone Acton 496, Ring 22.

By stating that Bellows Farm was for "nervous, tired people," and "operated by young people," he was broadening his customer base and opening the door to alcoholics from afar who needed to get away.

When Dropkick Murphy first opened his sanitarium, he welcomed both male and female alcoholics. But he and his wife weren't prepared for the romances that blossomed among the patients. Devoid of alcohol, and free of work and other obligations, many patients redirected their passions toward the opposite sex. The ever-changing population of patients, the budding relationships between them, and the drama that ensued as a result proved to be too much to bear for Murphy's wife, Marie. She decided it would be best to move away from the coed model of care and make Bellows Farm a place for men. One day, she pulled her husband aside and told him so. "It's either them, or me," she said.

To Murphy, the decision had been made.

"We gave the women the vamoose," he said.

8

WAR TIME

We make a living by what we get,
but we make a life by what we give.
—Winston Churchill

World War II was a turning point for many of Dropkick Murphy's mat colleagues, particularly Kaimon Kudo.

Kudo was from Fukushima, Japan, but spent most of his life in the United States. He was fifteen years old when he sailed from Japan and arrived in Tacoma, Washington, in March 1922.

Kudo and his wife were in Honolulu when Pearl Harbor was attacked by Japanese planes that roared across the sky. During the surprise ambush, a 1,760-pound bomb was dropped on the *USS Arizona*, resulting in a massive explosion that killed 1,177 crewmen. The *USS Oklahoma* was struck by torpedoes and capsized, leaving over four hundred men trapped inside.

Within hours of the attack, Hawaii was placed under martial law. Hawaii was still only a territory of the United States (it wouldn't become a state until 1959), and it would remain under military rule for nearly three years. Strict curfews were put into place, and there were mandatory "blackout" periods when no one could turn on any lights of any kind.

During World War II, the United States forced many people of Japanese descent to move out of their homes and into internment camps. Although internment was less common in Hawaii, it was clear that the government viewed residents of Japanese descent with suspicion. Japanese-language schools in Hawaii were forced to close, and residents of Japanese descent had earlier curfews. Hawaiian residents over the age of six had to be fingerprinted and carry identification at all times. Japanese-born citizens like

Kudo weren't allowed to travel to the mainland either (if he did, he would have risked being locked up in an internment camp).

In the years leading up to the war, Kudo had established himself as a national wrestling star who toured all over, from Kentucky to New York City to Washington to Chicago to San Francisco. But travel restrictions that were put into place essentially put a halt to Kudo's pro wrestling career.

Wrestling in Hawaii also suffered with the outbreak of the war. Two days after the attack on Pearl Harbor, the *Honolulu Star-Bulletin* reported that sports on Oahu were "practically at standstill." Wrestling promoter Al Karasick announced that the city's major wrestling venue—the Civic Auditorium in Honolulu—should be used for emergency purposes, and he canceled all wrestling shows until further notice. Kudo signed up for volunteer work, just like many of the other wrestlers who performed in Honolulu.

Throughout the 1940s, Dropkick Murphy continued to wrestle and develop his detox center.

In May 1942, Murphy appeared in a series of shows with Gus Sonnenberg. One of those shows was on Wednesday, May 13, at the Boston Arena. Paul Bowser organized the show and promised to give a portion of the proceeds to the athletic fund for the 22nd Coast Artillery at Camp Langdon, New Hampshire. The money would be used to buy boxing gloves, ping-pong tables, and other sports equipment for soldiers to use. Close to four thousand people attended and watched Dropkick Murphy and "Dynamite Gus" tussle for twenty minutes to a draw. In the main event, Steve "Crusher" Casey (who was stationed at Camp Langdon) beat Maurice "The Angel" Tillet for the AWA World Heavyweight title.

A few months after he wrestled Murphy in 1942, Sonnenberg joined the Navy. He became a chief specialist in the athletic branch and taught hand-to-hand combat and wrestling at Norfolk Naval Training Station in Virginia and the Navy school for physical instructors at Bainbridge, Maryland.

On Wednesday, November 11, 1942, Murphy wrestled on a card with one of his old mat colleagues, Winn Robbins. They wrestled at the Boston

Arena with Maurice "The Angel" Tillet and Danno O'Mahoney. Robbins drew his twenty-minute match with Everett Kibbons, and Murphy drew Paddy Mack.

☘ ☘ ☘

A couple of weeks later, on November 28, 1942, Robbins was working his other job at the Boston Fire Department. It was Saturday night, and Robbins was a rookie firefighter assigned to Engine Company 21, and his home base was the fire station on Columbia Avenue in the Uphams Corner section of Dorchester. That evening, at 10:20 p.m., the men noticed an alarm was struck at the corner of Church and Winchester streets. Because of the location, the company didn't have to respond to the call, but they noted the location and time of the alarm in the company journal. Three minutes later, a third alarm was struck from the same location. As men scrambled to put on their firefighting gear, they heard a fourth alarm.

Robbins, the hoseman for Engine Company 21, hopped on the back step of the hose wagon and held on tight as the fire engine sped down Tremont Street, turned onto Church Street, and then turned right onto Piedmont Street. Robbins and his colleagues jumped off the truck, picked up a hose, and started running toward the front door of the Cocoanut Grove nightclub.

Located at 17 Piedmont Street in the Bay Village section of Boston, the Cocoanut Grove was one of the most popular nightclubs in the city. The place was decorated like a tropical paradise, with artificial palm trees and coconuts. Patrons went there for drinks, dinner, and dancing.

What firefighters saw when they arrived would haunt them for years to come.

Robbins recalled the scene vividly. "When we first pulled in there was a woman in a red dress, evidently dead, lying in the gutter. There were a lot of dead people."

Robbins said their skin was blackened and charred.

Robbins and his fellow firefighters put masks over their faces and went inside, through the revolving door, where they encountered a gruesome scene. Human limbs were sticking out all over the place. "It was knee deep in bodies and they were like jackstraws, arms and legs and hands," Robbins would later recall.

Robbins had to climb and step carefully over the bodies to get inside. He and the other firemen made their way through the foyer and to the right, up a couple of stairs that led to the Caricature Bar, where they found even more victims. It was a ghastly sight. "They were all jammed up in there in panic," said Robbins. "And some of the people's heads were right through the first section of the wall, like through the plaster, and the people sitting on the stools at the bar as if they were still drinking there, but they were suffocated."

Robbins and other firefighters solemnly carried out burned bodies, one by one.

The firefighters opened the door to a telephone booth, where they found the body of a well-dressed woman inside. Her skin and clothes were intact. She wore a black fur piece around her shoulders. Apparently she died before making a phone call. A nickel lay on the floor of the booth at her feet.

The poor woman in the phone booth was one of 490 people who died as a result of the fire, one of the deadliest in American history. It was a night that Winn Robbins—and many other Bostonians—would never forget.

With each passing year, more and more of Murphy's mat colleagues made the transition from wrestling full time to other occupations. Many turned their attention to the war effort.

The war also impacted Jumpin' Joe Savoldi. The Notre Dame alum had achieved national fame and was launching a branded low-sugar energy drink called "Dropkick" when the war broke out. The mandatory rationing of sugar forced him to shutter his fledgling beverage business. And then the government came knocking. The Office of Strategic Services—the forerunner to the Central Intelligence Agency—wanted him to become a spy.

Jumpin' Joe Savoldi ended up joining the Office of Strategic Services. Savoldi had been born in Italy and lived there until he was twelve, so he was quite familiar with the country and the language. The U.S. government put his knowledge to use by making him a spy.

During one mission in 1943, Savoldi was working undercover behind enemy lines in Italy when his team found themselves surrounded by a barrage of mortar and shell fire. They slept in a bombed-out building in

Salerno and were awoken to the rapid-fire sound of German machine guns blasting through the city streets. When it was time for them to leave, they had to get to a breakwater that went three-quarters of a mile into the harbor. A British boat would be waiting there to pick them up. Germans stationed in the hills saw the group and aimed their 88mm guns at them, firing simultaneously. Each heavy blast was followed by another, and another, and another. Shells hit the water all around them. A British motorboat cut a jagged course through the water and reached them just in time.

While Savoldi was carrying out secret missions in enemy-controlled territories, other pro wrestlers found their niche stateside, teaching self-defense skills to soldiers. Ed Don George taught hand-to-hand combat to cadets at the U.S. Navy Pre-Flight School at Chapel Hill, North Carolina. World champion Lou Thesz was drafted by the Army and taught a similar course to soldiers at Fort Lewis, a military facility near Tacoma, Washington.

On Tuesday, August 14, 1945, the typically quiet town of Acton erupted in celebration when President Harry Truman announced that Japan had surrendered. After hearing the news on the radio, residents ran into the streets and gathered in groups, talking among themselves, jubilantly expressing their surprise and disbelief that the war was finally—finally—over. Church bells rang out, and the air-raid alarm was sounded at Town Hall.

Dropkick Murphy had been planning to retire from wrestling. After completing his last match, he had continued to rebuff advances from wrestling promoters who wanted to lure him back into the ring. One cloudy Monday in September 1945, Murphy decided to make his decision official on a piece of paper adorned with his own personalized letterhead. In an elegant Olde English font, the bold letters atop the page read:

BELLOWS FARM, DAVIS ROAD, ACTON, MASSACHUSETTS. TELEPHONE ACTON 496-22, P.O. ADDRESS: CONCORD, MASS. R. F. D.

Outside, the skies above Bellows Farm were overcast and gray. A storm was coming. That night, a cold rainy nor'easter hit Massachusetts. The wind howled.

Using a typewriter, Murphy wrote a letter to Jack Pfefer, the colorful wrestling promoter who was always looking to bulk up his stable of grapplers.

Dear Jack;

I was more than glad to get your most recent letter and also all the other folders which you have been sending. We are always glad to learn that you are doing well and follow your career with interest.

I regret that I will not be able to accept your offer to come to California and wrestle but it is not possible. As a matter of fact I am afraid that I will never wrestle again. Our business here is such that I think those days are over. I have not been inside a ring since February.

I now run a Health Farm, on the same line as Bill Brown's, and am quite pleased and proud that we are operating with from eighteen to thirty men here all the year round. We have had over 400 men here since March first. I employ eight people and in spite of the fact that you once predicted that I would never be a businessman I think I have come close.

So, Jack, while I sometimes miss the roar of the crowd and the excitement that went with the wrestling business it is a pleasure to be my own boss. Marie and I wish you all the success in the world and we do not forget that you helped in a large measure when we were trying to pile away a little bundle to buy this Farm.

Sincerely,
John Murphy

Murphy looked over what was effectively his letter of resignation, and announcement of his retirement from the ring, and sent it off to Pfefer. A new phase in his life was about to begin.

Dynamite Joe Rindone, a middleweight from Roxbury, came out to Dropkick Murphy's farm in Acton to train for his fight against Irish Bob Murphy at Braves Field in July 1951. Murphy, a light-heavyweight southpaw from California, won the bout and was later named one of *The Ring* magazine's 100 greatest punchers of all time. *Courtesy of David Murphy*

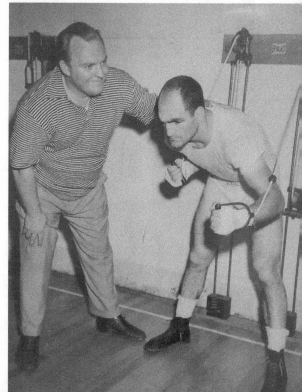

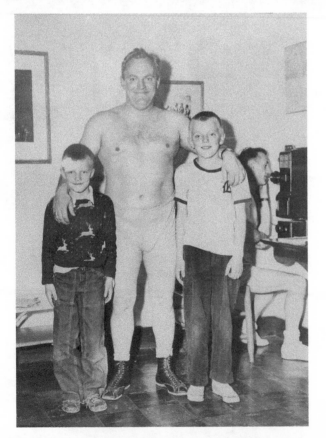

Frank Nichols (left) and Dropkick Murphy (far right) lend a hand to Sean, Tim, and Paddy, three boxing brothers who were known as the "Fighting Regans." They traveled from their native Ireland to launch their pro boxing careers in Boston in 1949 and trained at Bellows Farm. *Courtesy of David Murphy*

Dr. John "Dropkick" Murphy with two of his sons, David (left) and Richard (right) at Bellows Farm in Acton. The fellow talking on the telephone behind them is Boston Marathon legend Johnny Kelley. *Courtesy of David Murphy*

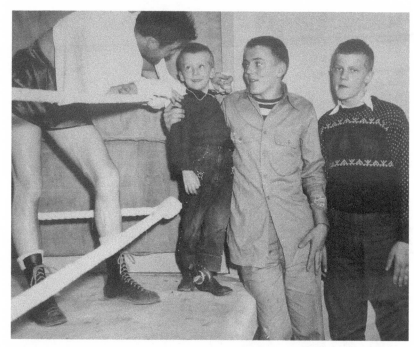

Tommy Collins paused his work in the ring at Bellows Farm to chat with Dropkick Murphy's sons Johnny, Dick, and David. *Courtesy of David Murphy*

Tommy Collins trained at Bellows Farm before his historic fight against lightweight champion Jimmy Carter at Boston Garden in 1953. *Courtesy of David Murphy*

Bull Curry. *Courtesy of Scott Teal/Crowbar Press*

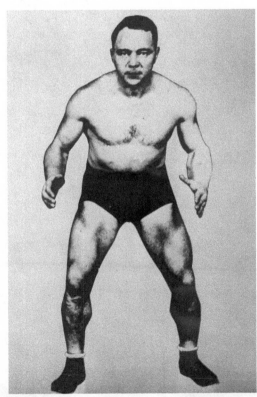

Gus Sonnenberg. *Courtesy of Scott Teal/Crowbar Press*

Ed Don George.
Courtesy of Scott Teal/Crowbar Press

Dropkick Murphy wrestles an opponent in these
undated photos. *Courtesy of David Murphy*

Courtesy of David Murphy

9

LIFE AND DETOX

It's screamin' and yellin' and swearin,'
all day long . . . everybody . . .
—Bobby Byrne, describing his stay at
Dropkick Murphy's sanitarium

D ropkick Murphy successfully made the transition from professional wrestler to health-farm operator. For many alcoholics, Bellows Farm was a place of refuge, a patch of high ground, if you will, amid a sea of drunken desperation.

The barn was the centerpiece of Murphy's sanitarium. It was well-preserved and painted a bold shade of red, like a fire engine, with bright white trim. A truly unique ornament adorned the rooftop of the barn: a one-of-a-kind personalized weather vane shaped in the likeness of Dropkick Murphy. His miniaturized muscular frame was parallel to the ground, floating in midair while performing a dropkick. His toes pointed in the direction that the wind was blowing.

The front lawn and side yards were meticulously landscaped. Murphy could often be seen there, mowing the lawn or watering the grass.

One day, Murphy hung a sign above his office door in the barn. In bold letters it read: IITYWIIWYBMAD.

All the regular patients knew what the sign meant. It became something of an inside joke. Newcomers would inevitably ask what the nonsensical jumble of consonants and vowels meant. Eventually, Dropkick or someone else would explain it was acronym that stood for "If I Tell You What It Is, Will You Buy Me A Drink?"

✽ ✽ ✽

Every car destined for Bellows Farm would drive along Route 2 and then turn right onto Davis Road. The car would then turn into the driveway lined with tall evergreen and sugar maple trees. Surrounded by the quiet countryside, the men at Bellows Farm would hear the noise of a car engine approaching. It was a warm, familiar sound that would grow louder and louder as it made its way up to the red barn. Men sitting outside would pause reading their newspapers and playing cards to glance at the new arrival. Sometimes it was a newcomer. But quite often it was a familiar face. If that were the case, the men outside would usually hoot and holler, greet their cohort with a hearty hello, and call out their name. *Hey Joe, you're back!*

The wobbly-kneed passenger would then be led inside the red barn. If they were in really rough shape and their mind was completely scattered, they might vomit and collapse into a chair. If they were aware of their surroundings, Murphy would check them in. The clients would take their watches and jewelry off and place their valuables in a box for safekeeping during their stay. One time a client checked in his false teeth. Clients would then be given a set of red pajama pants and a red sweatshirt—that was the standard-issue Bellows Farm uniform that patients wore.

Inside the barn, every inch of woodwork was completely pockmarked and covered with cigarette burns. Men would sit at tables shuffling and dealing cards, puffing on cigarettes, and reading newspapers.

Bellows Farm boasted an array of amenities. There was a solarium, as well as a massage room, and a billiards room where men could shoot pool. The gymnasium had state-of-the-art equipment, including a vibrating belt machine, used to shake and (supposedly) slim down the waistline. The gym also housed a regulation-sized boxing and wrestling ring as well as a steam room.

Dropkick Murphy also offered use of his facility to the public. On April 15, 1948, a large advertisement appeared in the local newspaper announcing that the gymnasium was ready for anyone to use:

Announcement!
Now open to the public

Dropkick Murphy's Bellows Farm Gymnasium is now open offering a complete program of physical reconditioning. We have the facilities and the "know-how" to make being healthy a lot of fun!

Our methods are not strenuous—just sensible. In addition to supervised exercise we stress physical activities [such] as handball, volleyball, badminton, weight-lifting, boxing, wrestling, etc.

A medically supervised hydrotherapy department offers a steam bath, electric cabinet solarium, showers, salt rubs and an expertly staffed massage room.

Whatever Your Own Program—to reduce or gain weight—to tone up the body—or just to relax—the Bellows Farm affords every modern convenience for your needs.

Open Daily 1 p.m. to 10:30 p.m.
Including Sundays

Murphy usually had thirty patients staying at the farm under his care. And if you counted the people who worked there, the athletes who trained there, and Murphy's family and friends, the property was often buzzing with activity.

Murphy's son, John Murphy Jr., once said: "I think some would come just to get away from it all. Out here, they don't have to worry about anything."

Bellows Farm employed a staff of about twenty people, which included doctors, nurses, dieticians, cooks, and maintenance workers. There was a masseuse, whom everyone nicknamed "Eddie the Rubber."

An unofficial mascot of Bellows Farm was a cat everyone called "Blackie." The cat had a piece missing from one of its ears, from fighting off another cat or some other animal, and enjoyed hanging out on the porch. John Jr. recalled that the men took a liking to the feline. "They used to give him bits of alcohol here and there," he said.

Reinert Anderson was the resident dishwasher. He started working there in 1940, the very beginning, and never left.

Arthur F. Desmond was the business manager at Bellows Farm. He was an alum of St. Anselm's, and more than a decade older than Murphy. He lived in Wayland and was a veteran of World War I. He served on the Massachusetts Commission on Alcoholism and chaired the Central Service Committee of A.A.'s New England intergroup headquarters.

John Brooks was the resident barber on the farm. Everyone called him Brooksy. Brooksy had a barbershop in Concord Center. His wife worked at the farm, making beds. When patients sobered up enough to care what they looked like, Brooksy gave them the old-school barber treatment. First he would place hot towels on their faces and then take a blob of thick white shaving cream and rub it all over their prickly, hair-covered cheeks and chin. Then he'd take a straight-edge razor and carefully scrape down their coarse stubble to a clean, smooth shave. In between each stroke down their cheeks and jawline, he'd dip the blade into a cup of water and tap it on the side of the cup. Then he'd pick up electric clippers—BZZZZ—and scissors—*snip, snip, snip*—and he'd cut their hair.

Freshly shaven and groomed, the clients would go get a massage from Eddie the Rubber and take a steam bath. They would then spend the next several days relaxing: reading the paper, playing cards, shooting pool, talking outside on the porch, smoking cigarettes, or watching TV. Before they left Bellows farm, they'd hand in their red uniform and get dressed in their own freshly laundered clothes; they would check out looking good, just like the "the businessmen, bankers, or whatever they were." The transformation in each patient's appearance, after a brief reprieve at Bellows Farm, always amazed Murphy's children.

Every man who walked through those doors went through a cycle. When they first arrived, they were often highly intoxicated. So typically the first stage was sobering up. Then there was the withdrawal stage. Sometimes they would shake and tremble. Some patients experienced anxiety, sweating, and nausea. Others developed visual and auditory hallucinations. Patients suffering from these symptoms of acute alcohol withdrawal were given medication on a set schedule.

After they checked into Bellows Farm, old routines (like going to the bar) would be replaced by new ones. Like the call for "prackie." At regularly scheduled intervals, men would congregate in the barn to receive their dose of medicine served up in a small shot glass. Newcomers got a shot of alcohol. Others got a shot of paraldehyde, a strong sedative that was used to calm down their alcohol-starved nerves. Everyone at Bellows Farm called it "prackie," and every day, each patient would sit and wait for their name to be called to receive their dose. It was a highlight of their day. They would tilt their head back and gulp it down. The stench was unforgettable and sizzled your nostrils. ("It was horrendous," recalled Murphy's son, John.)

Paraldehyde was a clear, flammable liquid that had a hot, burning taste. It was a drug that acted as a sedative and had been prescribed to alcoholics since the 1880s. It was also used to treat convulsive disorders.

The right dose of prackie slowed the patients down, made them drowsy, and relaxed their shakes enough so that they could get some sleep. It was potent stuff and gave them bad breath. First-timers sometimes endured a stomachache or felt nauseous. Less common side effects were clumsiness and hallucinations.

The dosing of medication was part of the daily routine. More experienced patients would look forward to their dose of prackie. Newer, bleary-eyed guests would sometimes beg for some regular booze. *Just a sip, Dropkick, just a small one, real quick . . . please, Dropkick. Please.*

Murphy would shake his head calmly and reply firmly. No. Some accepted his response better than others.

Murphy would instruct his patients to stick to the program and not drink on the sly, reminding them that mixing alcohol and medication was "dangerous business." Some patients were given limited amounts of alcohol, but only as prescribed.

"'Prackie,' I can still smell it a mile away—used to slow these guys down, all dreamy and beautiful," Murphy once said. "What booze was passed out was strictly on MD's orders and no fooling. A guy could be diabetic. He could be a pill-popper. You never knew for sure."

Doctor LeRoy P. Houck was the attending physician at Bellows Farm Sanitarium in the 1950s and '60s. He would make his daily rounds, checking on patients' blood pressure, heartbeats, and other vital signs. Born on July

25, 1921, in Pennsylvania, Houck served in the military in World War II and earned a purple heart and bronze star, lived in Concord in the 1950s, and worked as a family physician and a coroner for Middlesex County. He also worked at the Concord prison and was on the staff at Emerson Hospital.

Houck's son, Malcolm, recalled how his father would get called to Bellows Farm whenever new patients arrived:

> My dad was the last doctor in Concord to have his office in the front of the house . . . and he made house calls until the last day he practiced . . . but as a schoolboy many was the time when my dad was late from house calls for his evening office hours that I would answer his phone to hear male nurse Marty Duggan beller in his thick South Boston Irish accent: "Malcolm . . . tell yer fa-a-a-ther there's ten (or however many new admissions came in that day) at the Farm." Dad would take his evening office hours and then go to the "Farm."

One time Houck was a guest speaker on a panel addressing juvenile delinquency in Acton. Two hundred concerned parents attended the discussion, which was hosted by the Acton Parent Teacher Association in the cafeteria of the high school. Houck spoke of the dangers of excessive drinking and the dire consequences that followed. He had seen this first-hand, time and time again. "No young man ever thinks that he will die," he said. "Very few adults know it is possible to kill oneself with alcohol. I am not used to drinking alcohol and if I sat here and drank a pint of whiskey, either I would lose it or I would die. This is what happened to Dylan Thomas. He died of acute alcohol poisoning."

"Is there an answer to this problem?" someone in the audience asked.

Houck gave a straightforward response: "Set a good example for these youngsters, try to inform them of the consequences, try to protect them," Houck said, "and then hope."

Men came from all over—Nevada, Florida, Montana, and even Canada—to spend time at Bellows Farm Sanitarium. At least once a day a car would appear in the driveway to drop off a new patient.

"The full moon is always good for business," Murphy would say.

People would get dropped off by relatives. Sometimes they arrived in taxis. On at least one occasion, a patient got a ride in a police squad car.

It happened on a Wednesday morning, just after 6 a.m., when a gentleman who was making his way to Bellows Farm on foot decided he was too tired to continue. He stopped at Monument Square in Acton Center, ambled up beside a fire alarm box, and pulled the alarm. Police arrived on the scene first and found there was no fire—just a man standing beside the alarm, asking "rather dazedly" for a ride to Dropkick's. The patrol car promptly took the weary traveler to his destination. The very next day, the *Assabet Valley Beacon* newspaper ran an item on the incident on the front page. It was, according to the paper, the first time in Acton's history that the town's fire alarm system was rung and used as a taxi service.

Real cab drivers did get a lot of business out of Bellows Farm. Any taxi that traveled west on Route 2 beyond the Concord prison was almost certainly going to Murphy's farm, according to Malcolm Houck. Cabs would come all the way from Somerville, Charlestown, and South Boston, and if they appeared to be empty, it was usually because a passenger was lying down in the back seat "passed out or sleeping one off," he said.

When Robert Rhodes joined the Acton Police Department in 1961, the police station was located inside Town Hall. Cab drivers who lost their way would occasionally end up there.

"Once in a while a taxi would come by the station, at two or three in the morning, and come in and ask for directions," said Rhodes. "We'd know they were looking for Dropkick Murphy's."

Over the years, Dropkick Murphy paid his share of cab fares. One day a man who Murphy liked showed up in a taxi at Bellows Farm, asking for a favor.

"Pay the cabbie, will you Dropkick?"

"Okay," said Murphy.

Murphy went outside and walked over to the taxi idling in the driveway. He leaned his large frame over and looked inside the driver's window. The cabbie must have looked tired.

"What's the tab?"

"Two hundred and ninety bucks," said the cabbie.

Murphy's eyes widened in disbelief.

"Where in hell did you pick him up?"

"Charlottetown," said the cabbie. "Prince Edward Island."

Murphy shook his head and paid the driver. He then made a note of the unexpected expense, so he could bill his friend later.

One day a woman drove up Davis Road and parked her car. She had driven her husband all the way from Somerville. He was groggy and didn't know where he was. When he realized he was in Acton, at Bellows Farm of all places, he got out of the car, slamming the door with a heavy thud. He grimaced angrily and slapped his wife. She gasped. Murphy jumped up and tried to restrain him, but the man started to fight back. Then the woman took her pocketbook like a lasso and started swinging it, whacking Murphy in the head and back. "Leave my husband alone, you big bully!" she shrieked. All the men paused what they were doing and looked out at the commotion unfolding in the driveway. She pushed her husband back into the car and drove away.

Murphy never saw them again.

Over the years, Dropkick had his share of politicians saunter—and some-times stumble—into his establishment.

On one particular day, a limousine pulled up abruptly to Bellows Farm. The doors opened, and out tumbled a well-dressed politician, drunk out of his mind. He was a familiar face, a big-time politician. Everyone knew him, including Murphy. His handlers explained the situation: He had been playing golf in Dublin, Ireland. One too many drinks, he began get-ting drunk. His aide frantically placed a called to the State House seeking advice and was told curtly: "Bring him back—immediately."

The avid and inebriated golfer boarded a plane and flew across the Atlantic, landed at Logan Airport, and traveled in a limo to Dropkick Murphys.

The golfer was out cold. Twelve hours ticked by and his eyes fluttered open. He stretched his arms, yawned, looking for his clubs. "Who am I playing today?"

He thought he was still in Ireland.

Some patients wouldn't show up in Acton; they would get picked up. In those cases, Murphy would dispatch a driver—usually a staff member, or sometimes one of his sons—to go fetch a fellow perched on a stool at a darkened tavern.

These passengers sometimes had something to share with their chauffeurs. Murphy's sons recall them saying things like, "Your father is the greatest guy" or the ever-popular question, "Hey, can we stop?"

Sometimes, clients would ask to stop at Howard Johnson's restaurant in Concord, as it was the last establishment before Bellows Farm, and they served cocktails there. According to local lore, some men would be driven out that far, and then, after having their last hurrah at HoJo's, they would instruct the staff of the restaurant to call Dropkick if they passed out so they could get picked up.

Of course, Murphy's sons would not stop. Occasionally, when they said no, the passenger would get angry and say: "You're just like your goddamn old man!" or "I hate you and your whole family!"

Enduring such verbal assaults was part of the job.

You never knew who might be arriving, what they would act like, or how long they'd be staying. One thing was consistent though—men tried sneaking in liquor all the time.

Dropkick Murphy couldn't believe all the different ways that men attempted to smuggle booze into Bellows Farm.

"Some were bigger schemers than Ponzi," he once said.

But as much as Murphy despised this, he couldn't stay angry with the men, even if he tried. He loved the guys. He just didn't want them to put their health at risk.

Murphy recalled one particular time that an older gentleman stumbled out of a cab and staggered up the walkway in a crooked line, zigzagging in the direction of Marie Murphy. He stood before her, swaying slightly, and presented her with a bouquet of flowers.

While performing this gentlemanly gesture of chivalry, something unexpected happened. He bent over and took off his hat.

SMASH!

A half-pint bottle fell out of his hat and crashed down on the walkway.

Patients got creative in their games of hide-and-seek. They hid booze in trees and shrubs. They dug holes and buried bottles in the dirt. They tucked them into nooks and crannies of stone walls. One patient tried to hide hooch in hot-water bottles.

One lawyer who checked himself into Bellows Farm had a sports car that he parked nearby. A couple days into his stay, Murphy and his staff noticed that the lawyer was having difficulty responding to treatment; he seemed buzzed all the time, and it became clear that he'd been drinking. But where was he getting the booze? Murphy searched everywhere and couldn't figure it out.

One day, Murphy noticed a saucepan underneath the lawyer's sports car. He opened the petcock and alcohol started gushing out, splattering into the saucepan. The enterprising attorney had drained the radiator of his sports car and was using it as a personal storage tank for bourbon.

Murphy was always on the lookout for any contraband that might be hidden around his property. He also enlisted the help of his children to search the farm for liquor bottles that patients may have tried to stash away.

Malcolm Houck, whose father served as the attending physician at Bellows Farm, recalled how Murphy's sons would conduct a regular sweep of the property, "swishing through the tall grass with long sticks with a nail on the end," he said. "Every so often a telltale 'clink' would locate a bottle of whiskey."

Murphy's nephew, Jeff Allmon, remembers hunting for bottles with his cousin David Murphy. Their young eyes would sweep the grounds, looking in all the hollows of the ancient stone walls, searching for bottles hidden among rocks or stashed behind the wall, out of sight from the road. There was money to be made in this endeavor, too, as Murphy usually paid them for each bottle they recovered.

"We sort of knew, after a while, which patients coming in, if they had a bottle or not," he said.

In the morning, they would pay close attention to the patients checking in. "We'd see the new arrivals, and knew where to look," he said.

Every week they'd find two or three bottles. Each time they'd run back to Murphy and present their latest find, exchanging the bottles for some pennies, nickels, or a quarter.

As soon as he spotted a bottle, Allmon instantly thought, "a quarter!" Most of the time, after the patients sobered up, said Allmon, "they didn't even know they hid it."

Some men tried a different tactic. If they didn't smuggle in actual alcohol, they would try to keep some cash on them. "All the time, men were arriving, some with $10 bills glued to their mouths under dental plates," said Murphy, "so that maybe they could sneak out and buy a bottle when no one was looking."

Murphy recalled one time a patient took his red pajama pants off, sauntered down to the stable where Murphy kept his horses, opened the stable door, climbed on top of a horse, half-naked, and galloped away down Davis Road.

Dropkick Murphy had no idea this was happening, until the telephone rang.

Brrrrrrring!

Murphy picked up the phone. The voice at the other end was the owner of a local liquor store.

"Dropkick, you're not going to believe this, but a guy just came in, in his birthday suit, practically, and he bought two fifths, and he jumped on a horse outside and tore away. I think he's one of your guys."

Dropkick quickly hung up the phone, rushed outside and jumped into his car, and started driving. He hoped to cut the half-naked horseman off at the corner of Strawberry Hill and Davis Road. Sure enough, he spotted the pants-less patient on horseback, managed to corral him right then and there, and brought him back to Bellows Farm.

Years later, Murphy would tell the tale of how that infamous patient, wearing only a pajama top, "did a 'Hi-Ho Silver' down the road."

There were plenty of characters at Bellows Farm. Murphy himself once described the place as a "madhouse."

One man was fond of playing the ponies. Every afternoon, around the same time, he would track down Murphy and ask him to call a bookie and place a bet for him. Then he'd head upstairs to his room, sit down, and put his ear next to the radiator. He sat there enraptured, listening intently to the radiator. In his mind, he was listening to a horse race on the radio. Suddenly he'd get excited, hop up from his seat, and run downstairs with a piece of paper and a pencil in his hands, tallying up the money that he imagined he had just won.

Another patient, who had once been an actor, lived in constant fear of being electrocuted. He refused to sleep on a mattress because he was afraid of the coil springs, and made Dropkick take the bed out of his room. He would only sleep in a chair, dressed in rubber boots, a firefighter's rubber coat, and firefighter helmet. Just before he went to sleep each night, he'd take a small rug from the floor and drape it over his head.

One night a patient down the hall was suffering from delirium tremens, and he managed to get away from the attendant. He ran down the hall and went into the room of the actor, who had settled in for the night.

"Don't let him touch me!" the man pleaded with the actor, who was sitting in his chair with his firefighter gear on and the rug covering his face. "Please don't let him hurt me! If you don't stop him, he'll kill me!"

During this commotion, the actor calmly removed the rug off his head and replied, "I'm really sorry. I hope you don't mind—but I've given up making personal appearances."

One of Murphy's sons recalled an instance when a well-dressed patient stood out front, adorned in a suit, eyeing a small, round kiddie-sized pool that was on the lawn. It was just big enough to put your feet into. That didn't stop him from diving in. "Let's go for a swim!" he hollered, before falling into the little pool, fully clothed. He emerged victorious from the tiny pool, with water dripping from his completely drenched suit.

One memorable client earned the nickname "Willie the Pill" because he once plucked a pill from someone's vomit. Another patient kept a pet skunk. Another patient was obsessed with chopping down trees. This aspiring lumberjack ate a huge amount of oatmeal each morning and then went off into the woods with his axe and went to work, cutting down as many trees and shrubs as he could. He kept up this routine for years. Dropkick Murphy called him "the best worker I've got on the place— better than the hired help."

Murphy would climb into his enormously long station wagon to go to the post office, bank, and run other errands. Sometimes he'd take a few of the guys with him for the ride. On at least one occasion, they stopped at his son's baseball game at Middlesex School and cheered him on.

Many staff members of Bellows stayed there full-time. However, they would take a vacation every now and again. (Some of Murphy's children recall that the masseuse, Eddie the Rubber, and the carpenter would take off once a year to Canada where they would go on a bender in a shared motel room. Murphy would commission his oldest son Dick to go up there and bring them back.)

One day, a box arrived in the mail addressed to a patient. It smelled terrible. "His wife sent him her shit," recalled Dave Murphy.

One frequent patient was a Boston newspaperman who refused to wear the standard-issue red pajamas and insisted that he slept with his own clothes on: necktie, overcoat, and a Homburg hat. Lying in bed, staring at the ceiling, he was never without his formal felt headwear. Murphy called him "a big man with a pencil."

The frustrated newspaperman would pace up and down the hall, muttering under his breath. Sometimes he would glare at Murphy and bark: "Son of a bitch . . . get me a drink!"

The identity of the newspaperman Murphy described is not known. It is possible that he may have been David F. Egan, a renowned Boston sportswriter who wrote provocative columns under the pseudonym "The Colonel." He stood about five-foot-seven-inches tall, with a slight build, a high forehead, and a thin nose. He was well-dressed, tended to cross his legs whenever he sat down, and never backed down from anyone. He was also highly intelligent and an incredibly gifted writer, and his fleet-fingered writing prowess propelled him to stardom in Boston.

A native of Newport, Rhode Island, Egan finished his undergraduate studies at Harvard in just three years. After graduating cum laude in 1923, he went to Harvard Law School and came out with a law degree in 1925. While attending Harvard, he worked nights as an office boy in the *Boston Globe*'s library. He practiced law for one year and then returned to the *Globe* and began writing for the sports department. After twelve years at the *Globe*, he went to write for the *Boston American*, then did stints in PR for the Valley Arena in Holyoke and racetracks in Agawam, Rockingham, and Salem, New Hampshire, before returning to the newspaper business as a columnist for the Boston *Daily Record*. Egan had natural talent. He had fast fingers and an even quicker wit and turned out stories that hardly needed editing. His speed and talent made him the envy of the newsroom.

Egan was also never afraid of expressing his opinions, whether he was putting down Ted Williams or criticizing the racial segregation in baseball. In 1948, the NAACP honored him for voicing his support for having black players in the major league. The event was attended by 750 people, including the governor, mayor, and members of Congress. On October 23, 1948, the *Pittsburgh Courier* reported that Egan "has been wielding a cutting pen for years now, fighting for those in sports who have been persecuted for race, color, or religion. He's been particularly alert to the color problem and his bellows against the racial barrier in baseball made many a big-league owner run in a hole and pull his prejudice behind him."

Egan also had a drinking problem and paid his share of visits to Bellows Farm. In his biography of Ted Williams, author Leigh Montville recounted how Egan would go to Dropkick's to dry out, and there were stories that he would drive there in advance and hide bottles of booze in the trees and bushes. "He was an eminently resourceful drunk," wrote Montville.

✽ ✽ ✽

Another well-known figure who reportedly stayed at Bellows Farm was Joseph Sylvester Banfield, the alleged getaway driver in the infamous Brink's Robbery.

Banfield was a middle-aged ex-con who drank a lot. The guys in the Brink's gang called him by his nickname, "Barney," and his alcohol consumption took a toll on his body, mind, and overall appearance. His hair was dark and his skin pale. He parted his hair in the middle, but not particularly neatly. His face was soft and pudgy, with big round cheeks, a prominent double chin, and a thick neck that nearly poured over his shirt collar. His eyelids drooped slightly, as if he were missing some much-needed sleep, and the corners of his mouth turned downward like an upside-down letter "u"—the exact opposite of a smile.

Banfield was from Charlestown, a tight-knit and compact urban Boston neighborhood that was cut off from the rest of the city. It was a working-class community that was overwhelmingly Irish. Banfield got into trouble early on and dropped out of school as a youngster. He drank heavily and had plenty of run-ins with the police.

With only an elementary school education, Banfield found his niche behind the steering wheel and became known as an able driver—a skill that came in handy when committing a crime. He listed his occupation as a truck driver and laborer, but he seemed to put more of his efforts into illicit activities. Breaking and entering. Larceny. Robbery. Car theft. According to the FBI, burglary was Banfield's specialty.

In April 1937, when he was twenty-six years old, he pleaded guilty to a charge of conspiracy to steal liquor from a warehouse in Waltham. It was a daring robbery with a large haul. It happened on the night of December 8, 1936, and the enterprising burglars used an electric saw to cut through two walls to get inside the warehouse. They then used a custom-built wooden chute to shuttle cases of liquor out of storage across a four-foot alley, and then packed it up in a getaway vehicle. The thieves ended up taking 170 cases of liquor valued at $7,500. A truck found at the scene of the crime turned out to be stolen, and inside detectives found a portable power saw, an electric drill, the wooden chute, and other tools.

The judge presiding over the case glanced down at Banfield's lengthy criminal record, which would have made any judge raise their eyebrows and shake their head. He sentenced Banfield to six months in prison.

But those crimes were nothing compared to the infamous Brink's Robbery on January 17, 1950, when a gang of masked men got away with $1.2 million in cash and $1.5 million in checks, money orders, and other securities. The FBI placed Banfield at the scene and determined that he had driven the robbers to the Brink's building in the North End and then picked them up on Prince Street after they looted the place.

When the authorities later questioned Banfield, he told police he had nothing to do with the robbery; he had gotten drunk on New Year's Eve and continued on a monthlong bender. He didn't have a specific alibi for the night of January 17, 1950, but he claimed that he was drunk the whole month of January, so he could not have possibly been physically or mentally capable of committing the crime, never mind driving a getaway car. That's what he claimed, at least.

But no one bought that explanation. Rumors swirled around Banfield, that he drove the getaway car for the Brink's job. One of his ex-girlfriends told authorities that she saw him on the night of the robbery, and he didn't appear to be drunk at all.

After the Brink's Robbery, Banfield listed his occupation as "hoisting engineer"—an interesting title, considering he'd been accused of lifting so many stolen goods and was implicated in the Brink's job, which was the most sensational heist of its time. Most of the Brink's loot was never recovered.

At Bellows Farm, Banfield was always chomping on a toothpick, and always looking over his shoulder.

Banfield died young, on January 28, 1955, in his native neighborhood of Charlestown. He was forty-five years old.

Specs O'Keefe, who participated in the heist and later turned informant, said Banfield never disclosed what he did with his share of the stolen money. In *The Crime That Nearly Paid*, a book about the Brink's Robbery that O'Keefe co-authored with Bob Considine, it says: "Banfield had died, apparently from natural causes—if the consumption of vast amounts of whiskey can be called natural. What was more, Banfield 'took it with him.' He died without revealing where he had planted his $100,000 or what was left of it. It lay somewhere, rotting."

Banfield's presence at Bellows Farm gave rise to rumors that some of the Brink's cash was buried on Dropkick Murphy's property, near the intersection of Route 27 and Route 2. If that was indeed the case, it may still be there.

✽ ✽ ✽

Murphy's son David would never forget the day Rocky Marciano showed up at Bellows Farm with Jackie Gleason.

He recalled it was a Sunday morning, and they arrived in a fancy car.

Around that time, Marciano was hosting a syndicated TV show called *Main Event,* and Gleason appeared on the show as a celebrity guest. Gleason and Marciano were friends off-camera, too: Jackie introduced Rocky to golf, and Rocky was showing him how to exercise and get in shape.

According to Dropkick Murphy family lore, Gleason told Dropkick that he wanted to work out with Marciano at Bellows Farm, so he could lose some pounds. The only thing was, he wanted the place to himself. The patients would have to go. He wanted his privacy.

Gleason asked Murphy if he could lease the whole place for six months.

Murphy politely declined his offer. First and foremost, Murphy knew he could never ask patients to leave his sanitarium—where would they go? It was against everything he believed in. And the way he saw it, if he gave up Bellows Farm for any period of time, it would kill his business and his reputation.

Dropkick's son, David, recalled his father weighing the options, pondering the question: "What would happen to the farm? Everyone would be gone."

And so Dropkick made the decision.

"My father said no, because after he was gone, he'd be left with nothing," recalled David.

It turned out to be a wise choice. Although Gleason never got to take over the sanitarium, he did leave a lasting mark on the place. After his visit, someone found a picture of Gleason dressed in red golf attire, and doctored the image to make it appear like Gleason was wearing Bellows Farm's signature red pajamas. The clever soul then wrote, "If they're good enough for him, they're good enough for you!" The picture of Gleason dressed in the red Bellows Farm uniform was put on display and quickly became a conversation piece at the farm. From that day on, many who saw it assumed that Gleason had been a patient at Bellows Farm at some point. To this day, the rumor still persists. If you ask certain old-timers in Acton about celebrities who have come through town, there's a good chance they'll recite the fictitious tale of how Jackie Gleason once checked himself into Dropkick's.

Bobby Byrne remembers the first time he checked himself in as patient at Dropkick Murphy's and seeing that picture of Jackie Gleason. All the patients loved that picture.

"Of course they liked the idea of Jackie Gleason having been there," said Byrne. "For some reason it gave some kind of panache to the place, the fact that a man as famous as Jackie Gleason would go there."

Gleason wasn't atypical for a Hollywood star. He had a tough childhood, dropped out of school, and hustled his way to a successful career on stage and screen. Gleason's brash demeanor resonated with the men who came to Bellows Farm.

"People loved him, especially drunks loved him," said Byrne. "He had a barroom mentality. He grew up on the streets of New York. He was a saloon guy . . . and there are saloon guys all over Dorchester, Jamaica Plain, and Southie . . . those are saloon guys."

There were plenty of those guys at Bellows Farm.

"Everybody had a nickname," said Byrne. "Narco Norman. Home-run Brady. One-eyed Murphy."

"Almost every name was Irish," said Byrne. "It sounded like the Dublin phone book."

Byrne said many of the men he met at Dropkick's were politically connected and had government jobs, working for the city, the state, or the MTA, which was Boston's public transportation system.

"Mostly decent guys, but they liked to drink, and it was a way of life," he said. "Maybe some of them were into crime and all that, but they all suffered the same thing."

And eventually they all paid the same price. Screaming, yelling, and detoxing . . . shaking, rocking, and rolling.

"It was an interesting place," he said.

Bobby Byrne came into this world at the tail end of Prohibition. He was born in North Dighton, Massachusetts, on January 19, 1933. His parents split up when he was very young, maybe three years old, and he was raised by his mother. He attended the Taunton schools, played basketball as a kid, and graduated from Taunton High School in 1951. After he turned eighteen, he "drove 3,500 miles in a shitbox"—a 1940 Mercury—to Los Angeles to meet his father face-to-face. His father was bartending at a tropical bamboo joint called Zamboanga. It was a tiki-style nightclub and lounge that billed itself as the "home of the tailless monkeys" and the "most beautiful Polynesian paradise in the United States."

Byrne finally met his father in person. The reunion did not go well.

Byrne decided to head back east to Massachusetts, where he enrolled at Stonehill College, a small Catholic college in North Easton that was founded in 1948 and had just turned coed. There, Byrne studied English, philosophy, and political science. It took him six years to finish his under-graduate coursework, but he did it, and he received his bachelor's degree in English in 1958. He went on to teach at Foxborough Junior High, then chased a girl to Florida and taught for a while in Miami, then at New Bedford High School back in Massachusetts.

Byrne was Hollywood handsome, with a square jaw and a cleft chin, and curly dark hair that he wore short, styled up in front and combed back on the sides. He looked like a member of the Rat Pack, framed by faint gray ringlets of smoke from a lit cigarette in his hand.

In 1965 Byrne went to New York and rented an apartment with three friends who worked as bartenders in Manhattan. Byrne taught one day at a public school in Bedford-Stuyvesant, a tough neighborhood in Brooklyn. Virtually all of his students were black. Some of them asked Byrne if he was a cop. He was teaching an eighth-grade class and one kid, in a Boy Scout uniform, ripped a desktop off and threw it at him. The next thing Byrne knew, he was in the principal's office.

"I think you should work in a parochial school, Mr. Byrne."

Byrne walked out of the school and never went back. Instead, he got a different job entirely, at a bar on the Upper East Side called the White Horse Tavern. A friend of his, who he knew from the Cape, worked there. It was located at 1713 Second Avenue, by 89th Street. The bar's slogan was "He who drinks water, thinks water." Norman Mailer was one of his customers.

Byrne loved literature. One of his favorite pieces was by Ernest Hemingway: "A Clean, Well-Lighted Place," a short story in which an old man seeks solace in drinking brandy at a cafe late at night.

Byrne talked like a writer, with wit and rhythm.

"The pub is all rhetoric and ragtime," he said.

"I was a pretty good bartender," he said. "There's a certain kind of grace in terms of the mechanics of it."

Byrne once wrote a manuscript, what he described as a "realistic novella," about his experience behind the bar. The story describes a typical night tending bar, and what he was thinking at the time.

Byrne speculated on the motivation and psychology of his customers and came up with a hypothesis of what attracted his customers to the barstools before him. "Man, for centuries, has been gathering at a log . . . to be together . . . wanting to be a part of something that's larger than what they are," he said.

He viewed the bar as an altar of sorts. Last call was like the end of mass. If you cut someone off, you were excommunicating them.

Byrne took solace in writing. "Art is redemptive. You can get a lot of mileage out of your mistakes," he said.

And Byrne admits he made quite a few of them. The first time he went to detox was in New York. He went because he had to—he was physically sick, suffering from acute gastritis, which meant his stomach lining was inflamed. He was in pain and unable to drink. His body began to rebel against him. Without the alcohol, he began suffering withdrawal symptoms and experiencing delirium tremens, also known as "the shakes," or "the DTs." He felt shaky and agitated. His limbs trembled.

"The DTs were no fun," said Byrne. "You shake and shake and shake and rattle and roll and your neck gets sore from shaking . . . it's just aggravating because you can't sleep. You're just shaking and just sometimes you're even hallucinating for a couple days. Not all the time . . . the hallucinations I had were . . . I dreamed there were like cats in the room or something like that. At least I never had a psychotic episode. . . . Every muscle gets sore, and it's just exhausting."

After that initial detox, Byrne would go on to many more detoxes—forty-two, to be exact.

The first time Byrne went to Bellows Farm was in 1968. He had to be detoxed again. He had been visiting his sister, who lived in Framingham at the time.

"My sister Bonnie took me to Dropkick's," he said.

Byrne recalls receiving a hearty welcome when he arrived at Bellows Farm. Guys were hollering out, greeting him.

"When you first arrive, there's a big porch in front of the building, and maybe thirty or forty crazy Irish people would be there clapping, applauding you, all wearing their red pajamas and their Bellows Farm Sanitarium shirts," he said.

"When you get there, they make you put on the red pajamas and the shirt. Of course you're kind of always drunk or sick when you go in there, at that point."

After checking in his belongings and changing into the standard-issue uniform, the next big step was receiving his first dose of paraldehyde. It was something that he, and the other patients, looked forward to.

"Everybody liked paraldehyde because it makes you sleep," Byrne said. "It didn't taste that terrible. You could mix it with orange juice. Or you could drink it straight. I didn't think it was bad. It's hard to describe the taste—it was a very medicine-like taste. It wasn't bitter or anything like that, like a lot of medicines are. . . . It was like drinking whiskey, but better. It was unbelievable; it was wonderful stuff, to tell you the truth," he said.

After imbibing the prackie, he felt better.

"You'd just relax," he said. "You'd be able to exhale. You wouldn't be so uptight. You'd be more pacific, more serene . . . and life wasn't that bad after that. People would just wander through everything, just . . . in a fog. It was almost like surreal at the time. There'd be people all zoned out with magazines upside down, not really reading them, just holding them waiting for the paraldehyde. That's how it went, every day for three and half or four days, they'd give you paraldehyde. Or if you had the DTs they'd give you Mt. Vernon Rye Whiskey, an ounce every hour, so you wouldn't go into the DTs.

If someone had the shakes really bad or needed time away from the rest of the patients, they had the option of taking a trip to a special room at Dropkick Murphy's that everyone referred to as "Little Tokyo." Byrne always wondered how it got its name.

"After the fourth day, [Murphy] would give you this concoction called Dropkick's Number 11, which I think was phenobarbital and water . . . a mild, mild, mild barbiturate . . . to get you prepared for the fifth or sixth day, when you were going to leave, so you didn't come out of there all goofed up," he said. "Phenobarbital had a milder effect."

Every night was the same. "You get a good sleep, and then when you wake up, then . . . I guess the day begins. Whenever you get up, they feed you, and it's all like screamin,' yellin,' and swearin' all day long—everybody. It was like a mad house," he said.

But it was a mad house in a positive sense. One would never feel lonely at Dropkick's.

"It was kind of an interesting poetic experience in a way . . . if you want to stretch the definition of poetry," Byrne said. "There were a lot of laughs, too, and a lot of insults, and camaraderie and those kinds of things."

Byrne would end up returning to Dropkick's again.

"In 1970 when I was there my sister and her husband came to New York to pick me up. Of course they were shit-faced when they picked me up; they enjoyed the little trip."

John and Bonnie lured Byrne with a "bait bottle" of booze.

His sister turned to him. "Do you want to go to Dropkicks?" she asked. "Yeah," he replied.

Bobby Byrne doesn't have many memories of that trip, "except drinking booze in their van on the way to Dropkick's."

Compared with other detox facilities, Bellows Farm "was almost resort-like," he said. "Dropkick's was the most fun, if you can use that word to describe the experience." Patients could walk around Bellows Farm freely if they chose, and without supervision.

Byrne knew what he was getting into when he went to Bellows Farm.

"You know ain't gonna get any ragtime, you ain't gonna get any pseudo-psychiatrists . . . young counselors that didn't know shit. No one was going to scold you. There was no moral component to it. You could go there and eat and have a little fun."

The atmosphere was casual and relaxed. "Because you knew there were going to be some kind of laughs, there'd be some camaraderie, and there'd be stories . . . and drunks love stories," Byrne recalled. "So there would be many stories there about guys talking about when they were young, and what they did, and screamin' and yellin' and rantin' and raving and tellin' tall tales, not different from the things that used to go on in mining camps and lumber camps where men gather around a common experience."

Think of guys working in Civilian Conservation Corps camps during the Depression, pioneers exploring the wilderness of the Yukon or heading west for the California gold rush, or hobos riding the rails all over the country. That's what Bellows Farm was like.

"A lot of poetry came out of those kind of experiences."

"So at Dropkick's, people would be talking that. They'd be talking ragtime and horseshit and enjoying it. Better than listening to some asshole scold you for what you did. . . . It was good theater."

Thinking of his times at Bellows Farm reminds Byrne of the song "Big Rock Candy Mountain" that Harry McClintock recorded in 1928:

In the Big Rock Candy Mountains
There's a land that's fair and bright

Where the handouts grow on bushes
And you sleep out every night

The song described a hobo's paradise, a place where the sun always shines, food is plentiful, and cigarettes grow on trees. That's how Byrne remembered his times at Bellows Farm. But every visit to Dropkick Murphy's eventually had to come to an end.

"Then they'd release you, and you'd pay your bill, and you'd have somebody pick you up, and then you'd have to go back and rebuild your life again . . . until the next detox," said Byrne.

It was a horrible cycle. One that Byrne came to know well.

Byrne still has the receipt from his first visit to Bellows Farm. At the top of the letterhead it says:

ESTABLISHED 1940

BELLOWS FARM SANITARIUM
40 DAVIS ROAD
ACTON, MASSACHUSETTS 01720

The date is typewritten: Sept. 24, 1968

Arrival: 9-18-68
Departure: 9-24-68

Admittance charge (7 days inclusive) $126
Medicine $17
Massage $8
Barber $1.50
Cigarettes $2.80
Telephone .40
Total $155.70

He also has a receipt from another visit he made, on Halloween night in 1970. At the top it says:

BELLOWS FARM HOSPITAL
BOX 231
ACTON, MASSACHUSETTS 01720

Nov. 7, 1970

Arrival: 10-31-70
Departure: 11-5-70

Room and board: $132
Medicine: $17
Cigarettes: .40
Telephone: .35

The total from that trip was $149.75.

Bobby Byrne keeps those receipts in a file folder labeled "Hard Times."

John "Doc" McNiff grew up in Acton and graduated early from Acton Boxborough Regional High School in 1964. He enlisted in the Navy and within two weeks of graduation was in boot camp.

After graduating from Hospital Corps School he was assigned to the Chelsea Naval Hospital in Boston, and from there he went to Field Medical School at Camp Lejeune, North Carolina, and then to Vietnam in May of 1966 with the Third Battalion Fourth Marines where he saw combat in several operations. McNiff returned to the United States in June 1967 and was discharged at Long Beach, California, in July 1968.

He returned home to Acton and joined the local police department that year. He was issued, like his fellow patrolmen, a six-shot .38-caliber Colt revolver.

Early in his law enforcement career, he worked as a patrolman for the Acton Police Department while taking classes at Northeastern. He also picked up some part-time work at Bellows Farm from 1969 to 1970 as a fill-in night nurse.

"By the time I met John he was very well-off, but he told me that when he arrived in Acton, he had $80 in his pocket," recalls McNiff. "He always drove a Ford Country Squire station wagon. He did this on purpose because, according to John, if you started to ride around in a flashy luxury car people would accuse you of forgetting where you came from."

McNiff worked for Murphy for a couple of years. "Nobody called him Dropkick to his face. But everyone knew him as Dropkick," he said.

There was a small office attached to the barn. That's where they locked up the medications and cigarettes and kept toothbrushes, toothpaste, and other necessities. One day the phone rang and McNiff picked up.

"This is Joe Louis. Is John there?" the voice on the other end asked. McNiff thought it was someone playing a prank. But it really was Joe Louis.

McNiff recalled how some new patients were initially placed in the Little Tokyo room. Little Tokyo itself was just a small room big enough for one bed. Inside the room it was dark. Dropkick "called it Tokyo because well, that's where they might as well be," said McNiff. "Whenever a guy showed up hammered, he'd put 'im in there until he slept it off."

At night McNiff would give out medication to the men before they went to bed. Some got a measured amount of whiskey. Others were given prackie. McNiff recalled that the prackie was served in a small glass tumbler and mixed with a bit of juice so it wouldn't taste as bad. "How they ever got it down, I have no idea," said McNiff.

"It was powerful," added McNiff. "It helped them sleep."

McNiff's shift typically ended at midnight, but Murphy often cut him loose early. McNiff was working two jobs and going to school and didn't get to see his wife much. "We'd argue through notes," he recalls.

"Many, many nights, [Dropkick would] stick a jug under my arms and say, 'here, now get off my property.' Or he'd say, 'take this home and see what you can do with it'. . . he was just that kind of guy."

McNiff found bottles lodged in the stone walls that lined the road up to Dropkick's. "There'd be a stone and a jug, a stone and a jug." McNiff would retrieve the bottles and turn them over to Dropkick. "It wasn't a popular thing with the patients," he said.

The food at Bellows Farm was also memorable, according to McNiff. Murphy's wife usually cooked for the men about once a week. The farm also employed chefs who prepared meals for the patients the rest of the time. The menu varied. Steak. Pork chops. Beans and franks. Spaghetti. Prime rib. Roast beef. Homestyle comfort food served to men with stressed-out stomachs and overtaxed livers who needed all the comfort they could get.

"DINNER AT THE HOUSE, BOYS!" Murphy would cup his hands around his mouth and yell. That was the signal for the men to put down their newspapers or playing cards or whatever else they were doing and head to the house for supper.

McNiff said one of the chefs who worked at Bellows Farm made excellent baked stuffed shrimp. The tender shrimp—butterflied lengthwise, cooked in butter and minced garlic—was the best McNiff ever had. And he'll never forget the day that chef died.

"As I remember it was a very hot day and I was sitting in the dining room/kitchen area when the chef walked by, sweating profusely," said McNiff. "When he came back, he got to about where I was sitting and collapsed. I caught him on the way down and lowered him to the floor. He was still conscious and had shallow breathing. He did not speak. We called the fire rescue—there was no 911 at that time—and they transported him to Emerson Hospital in Concord. The hospital called us later and told us that he had died."

"Maybe the Good Lord liked his shrimp too," McNiff speculated.

Brian Goodman was another Acton police officer who worked at Bellows Farm. In 1969 he joined the Acton Police Department, and as a junior police officer on the force, he was stuck with the midnight to 8 a.m. shift. Back then, patrolmen working the overnight shift would regularly pick up a newspaper and bring it to Dropkick's. Murphy, in turn, would chat with them and offer them a mug of coffee or a glass of soda. For the patrolmen, those visits to Bellows Farm were a nice way to break up the monotonous patrols of Acton's quiet, rural landscape. It was a dry town, and not much happened after dark.

One night, Murphy asked Goodman if he wanted to work for him on the side. It was a perfect opportunity to make some extra cash. From that point on, when he wasn't on patrol, Goodman worked part-time at Bellows Farm.

"I worked there in the early 1970s. I did maintenance, mowed the lawns, ran errands for him and used to pick up patients when they called."

More often than not, someone else—a relative or spouse—called Dropkick's and notified them that an alcoholic in their lives needed to dry out. Goodman and another person would take the station wagon and drive to wherever they were. It might be a house. It might be a barroom. Goodman traveled as far as New Bedford, which is 80 miles away from Acton, to pick up a patient.

You had to talk them into the vehicle. "They knew where they were going," he said.

"They had all kinds of people there . . . even priests," said Goodman.

Goodman remembers the experience of mowing the lawn and discovering nips of liquor scattered throughout the grass.

"You'd be driving along on the lawnmower, and BANG! You'd hit a bottle. You always knew what it was," said Goodman.

Goodman recalled that the food was top-notch—to him, the equivalent of a five-star restaurant.

After the initial shock wore off, the patients would get used to the slower pace of life in the country. But sometimes a patient wandered off. Occasionally they would start walking down the railroad tracks toward Lowell. If Murphy could not recover the patient himself, he would notify the police. Police in the neighboring communities of Lowell and Chelmsford usually picked up the patient and brought him back. They weren't hard to find because they were dressed in red pajamas.

Dropkick Murphy's policy was that patients were never held against their will; they could check themselves out and leave at any time.

"If they insisted on leaving, it was their choice," Murphy once said. "We cajoled, pleaded, and did a lot of things to convince them that they should stay. They were sick. But in the last analysis, it was their choice."

Police were rarely called to Bellows Farm. "We never got calls to go over there," said Goodman. "Dropkick took care of everything himself. When he spoke, people listened to him. He was stern, but nice."

♣ ♣ ♣

Thanks to Dropkick Murphy's Bellows Farm sanitarium, the little town of Acton learned more about alcoholism, and alcoholics, than many other communities of its size. But there was still a significant stigma attached to alcoholism.

Frank Anthony, a columnist at the *Assabet Valley Beacon*, was unsympathetic. On May 23, 1968, he wrote a column titled "Your Alcohol Is Showing." In that column, he declared that nondrinkers were looked down on when "in reality, it is the alcoholics who are the freaks." He blamed alcoholics for overwhelming hospitals "to the point where doctors have lost their zeal for the practice of medicine." He also proclaimed that "there is more likely to be a predominance of alcoholics in a social-climbing town or a drinker's haven like Concord, where the socialite ladies get together for alcohol in the morning rather than coffee, than there is in a workingman's town like Maynard, where the lights of many liquor establishments outshine all other types of business."

Anthony then went on to describe, in his opinion, the common behaviors of alcoholics. "With the ladies there is a tendency to talk too much and be too aggressive ... a problem that has grown since they got the right to vote and ruined the political system," he wrote. "Men display their alcoholic problem with foul language, dirty jokes, and boisterousness."

It was a provocative column, indeed, and one that Dropkick Murphy's daughter-in-law couldn't let go. On May 29, 1968, readers of the *Assabet Valley Beacon* turned to the second page and found a letter to the editor from Dropkick Murphy's daughter-in-law. The headline above the letter stated plainly, in bold black letters: **Rebuttal to Frank Anthony.**

Mr. Frank Anthony
"One Voice"
Beacon Publishing Co.
Maynard, Mass.

Dear Mr. Anthony,

Many times in the past I have been irritated by various remarks you have made in your column, "One Voice," but your latest outburst in the May 23, 1968, issue of the Assabet Valley Beacon *is one that I cannot let pass without a rebuttal. Your outrageous inaccuracies, vague generalities, and insulting innuendoes demonstrate not only a profound ignorance of alcoholism, but also a childish vindictiveness that I feel is not worthy of a man of your supposed intelligence.*

First of all, you have no conception of what an alcoholic is. You seem to presume that anyone who drinks alcoholic beverages is an alcoholic, which you must realize is a ridiculous idea. A great majority of people in our society drink, often in moderation and occasionally in excess, without ever becoming alcoholics. Sometimes the difference between a heavy drinker and an alcoholic may appear to be so slight as to be nonexistent, but there IS a difference. One Alcoholics Anonymous definition of an alcoholic is a person who has a "physical compulsion, coupled with a mental obsession" to drink.

Secondly, I would like to take issue with your often repeated statement that alcoholics are "freaks." Would you call a cripple, an epileptic, or one with cerebral palsy a "freak" also? Alcoholism is not a moral or social problem, but a medical one. The American Medical Association stated in 1956 that alcoholism is an illness, a progressive and incurable disease. It is an illness which, like cancer for instance, happens to some people but not to others. No one knows why this is so, but a great deal of research is being done now to try to determine the reasons, and we can only hope that someday a real cure will be discovered.

Thirdly, I cannot agree with your statement that alcoholics have "overloaded our hospitals . . . to the point where doctors have lost their zeal for the practice of medicine." If this were true, then it would also be true of people afflicted with cancer, or mental illness, or any other disease for which a cure has not yet been found. Can you name even ONE doctor who feels this way? I doubt it. Working with alcoholics can certainly be quite frustrating, but even a few successes can make it worthwhile.

I do agree with you on one point, that those who drink should not drive, but non-alcoholics who drive "after a few" drinks cause many more accidents than the relatively small number of alcoholics who drive while on a "bender." These non-alcoholics are especially dangerous because they don't realize what "just a few" drinks can do to their reflexes, or how they can impair their judgement, so that they are apt to be quite reckless behind the wheel.

Another statement that you profess to be a fact is that there are more alcoholics in Concord than there are in Maynard. I would like to know where you found statistics to prove this, since I am quite sure that this is not so. If it were possible to conduct a survey, I think you would find there are just as many alcoholics per capita in Maynard as in Concord. Alcoholism is not a disease of just one class, but of all classes, including blue-collar workers, white-collar workers, executives, the "idle rich," and just the idle. I object to your insinuation that the people of Maynard are the only ones who drink beer and watch the Red Sox on TV. I am sure that many Concordians also enjoy this pastime, as well as Actonians, and even those who live in Stow.

You seem to think that an alcoholic is an object of amusement, a figure of fun. Let me tell you that an alcoholic is neither "quaint" nor "amusing" as you so blithely put it. It is very obvious that you have absolutely no understanding of this disease, and therefore you should not judge alcoholics so harshly. Instead of condemning THEM, you should condemn society for making it so difficult for an alcoholic to remain sober. Alcoholics need constructive help and intelligent criticism, not malicious ignorant attacks in the mass media.

If you are sincerely interested in doing something about alcoholism, I suggest that you first learn something about it. I am enclosing several pamphlets put out by Alcoholics Anonymous, which can give you a good idea of the complexities of alcoholism, as well as some of the ways A.A. helps problem drinkers. I do hope you will read them carefully and with an open mind. If you are not interested in learning about alcoholism, then I would suggest that you NOT use your column in the Assabet Valley Beacon *to spread your biased opinions to its thousands of readers. After all, you have certain responsibilities as a columnist which should not be taken lightly, and which should include knowing what you are talking about, and not distorting facts to fit your personal opinions. I think you have done a great disservice to the readers of the* Beacon, *and especially to the many members of A.A. in this area, as well as to their families.*

In conclusion, Mr. Anthony, I would like to paraphrase the last sentence in your column: Your ignorance is showing.

Sincerely,
Mrs. Richard H. Murphy
Bellows Farm Sanitarium
40 Davis Road
Acton, Mass.

When Anthony read her letter, he felt compelled to respond and wrote a rebuttal of his own for his next column, which appeared in the June 6, 1968, edition of the paper:

ONE VOICE
By Frank Anthony

I am flattered that Mrs. Murphy stated in her letter to the editor last week she has "been irritated many times in the past" by my columns; and although she has indeed put the overalls in her own chowder, it was a pleasant surprise to have such a strong reaction to my recent column on alcoholism.

Little did I realize that some people feel so protective toward people who, by one means or another, fall into the trap of alcoholism. There are, of course, those who feel justified to rationalize drug addiction and the excessive use of nicotine or even caffeine as incurable. The rationale is the same i.e., these indulgents are not to blame for what they do . . . it is an "illness." They are only "sick." There are many degrees of this problem. Mrs. Murphy's interest seems to be only in the "incurable." If I were interested in defending the libelous attempt to label my interest in the growing threat of alcoholism as "ignorant," I could publish a list of doctors who have expressed their concern to me about the overwhelming numbers of people who occupy hospital beds due to the excessive use of alcohol and nicotine.

I only answer this letter in the hope that it will help general understanding in the whole area of personal excessive abuse of the body . . . in particular the use of alcohol. One can, of course, understand the interest of people who run sanitariums, but there is the very real lack of public interest in this problem which is growing daily in high school and home.

I do not agree that alcoholics or drunks are not responsible for what they do any more than I would agree that sex perverts should be sympathized with and excused for killing or violence because they are "ill" and do not know better. People are not born ill. They become that way for a variety of reasons, not the least of which is the massive overkill of sex, alcohol, and nicotine they ingest as their daily diet from mass media.

With the recent use of psychology and the social studies there is a growing tendency to "understand" these personal abuses and excuse them as an "illness." This is less than comforting to parents, or loved ones, of those who are victimized by the acts of such "sick" people.

And, unless such excessives (if one would rather call them that instead of freaks or radicals) are held personally responsible for their conduct and condemned, the whole nation which tolerates such people will become just as "sick."

There are many examples, too numerous to mention, of these situations in all walks of life. I know a congressman who continues to spend many years in Washington (and who is a known alcoholic) as long as he pleases a sufficient number of the voters he will remain in Washington bars until he passes away or is pushed out of office at the ripe old age of 80 or more.

The former husband of a divorcee holds a "highly sensitive" position in the state department. She asked me last week how they can keep a known alcoholic in such a position and expect him not to be a risk.

A division head of one of our largest industrial plants has destroyed many fine young men below him in the ranks. Even though an alcoholic, he remains in his position, gathering only weak subordinates around himself as the company suffers because of it.

A teacher of school children, at a highly sensitive age level, remains on the job for year after year while hundreds of parents wonder why their school children falter and fail under the influence of that particular person, at that particular grade level. I could go on for a book's length as any writer can who has traveled broadly, lived in various parts of the land and known many people. The fact remains, as long as alcoholics are tolerated in these important places it is the children, the people and the very nation itself which suffers as a result. And for every alcoholic there are dozens around him who suffer.

Most important of all, it is these very same people who are responsible for saying nothing while the alcoholic steers the automobile, the child or the country toward a collision.

When one gets to the point where such lack of personal responsibility is excused as illness, then it is time for those who make the excuses to examine their own logic.

Over the course of operating Bellows Farm, Murphy raised seven children: Richard, Dave, John, Marie, Michael, Susan, and Amy. They had an uncommon childhood.

Murphy said the patients never bothered his children, and vice versa. He said his children understood that the men were sick and treated them with dignity and respect.

"Funny thing, I think being here gave my kids compassion . . . my kids never looked down their noses at these men," Murphy said.

Bellows Farm was an interesting place to grow up. Some of the older Murphy boys would go over to the tracks and dare each other to place pennies on the rails. They spent countless hours running around in the woods and swimming and fishing in Nashoba Brook. They explored the ruins of the old pencil factory. Another favorite spot in the woods was an old stone chamber that was built into a slope overlooking Nashoba Brook. The kids would ride along in their yellow Coot, an early all-terrain vehicle that was patented in the late 1960s. It had four-wheel drive and a body that could twist and turn to get over tree stumps and brush.

Murphy's youngest daughter, Amy, would make forts out of empty cardboard boxes. She and her siblings scurried up onto the roof and hid out, trying to stifle their giggles while watching the men below. They played wiffle ball in the barn; whenever the ball hit the ceiling, it counted as a home run.

Dropkick Murphy's nephew, Jeff Allmon, has fond memories of playing with his cousins at Bellows Farm.

Allmon's father died at a young age, when his submarine was sunk in the Pacific Ocean during World War II. After the death of his father in 1942, Murphy offered his mother a bookkeeping job at Bellows Farm. Jeff and his mother moved to Acton, and their house was only about a mile from Bellows Farm. Jeff spent a lot of time at the farm playing with his cousins while his mother worked.

"We had free rein over everything . . . we did what we wanted," he said.

They ran through the woods, played in the creeks. Allmon recalls very little adult supervision. "It was a great life," he said. The only place that was off-limits was the second floor of the barn; that's where unruly patients were kept.

His mother ended up falling in love with a patient at the farm. When Dropkick learned of their relationship, he was "totally opposed to it," Allmon recalls. But the patient stopped drinking completely, and they ended up staying together. They got married and raised five children together. Allmon said when his stepfather died, he had been sober for fifty-five years.

As a youngster, Dropkick Murphy's oldest son, Richard, forged a deep connection to the land in Acton, and as an adult, he devoted much of his time and energy to maintaining and preserving the woodlands along Nashoba Brook, which ran through the Murphy family's property.

Hundreds of years before, Native Americans set up campsites along the banks of Nashoba Brook and constructed weirs to catch fish. Later on, in the 1700s and 1800s, white settlers harnessed the waterpower of the brook and set up mills to grind flour and cut wood. Those early businesses eventually disappeared, but traces of their existence remained.

Richard would walk along the stream, clearing out trails around it and removing brittle branches and dead shrubs as needed. He enjoyed fishing and hiking and invited the public to enjoy what nature had to offer in his family's backyard. He welcomed trout fishermen to cast their lines into the stretch of Nashoba Brook that ran through their property. He researched the history of the farm and led groups on nature walks.

In 1958, Richard came up with a strategy to keep the stream clean. Over the next several years, the Murphys acquired all the undeveloped land from the dam at the end of Wheeler Lane to the Route 2A bridge. It was that foresight that saved Nashoba Brook from getting polluted, preserving it for generations to come.

Richard once wrote a letter to the editor of the local newspaper:

January 20, 1968
Mr. Earle Tuttle
Beacon Publications
Maynard, Mass.

Dear Mr. Tuttle,

On January 19, 1968, the League of Women Voters sponsored an "Evening with Conservation" at the Acton Boxborough High School.

At this meeting, an Acton resident asked if there were any areas left in Acton where a person could take an uninterrupted one or two hour afternoon walk through a woodland area. He was told there was not.

However, there is one such area left. The woodlands owned by Bellows Farm in North and East Acton have always been open to conservation-minded groups or individuals.

Sincerely,
Richard Murphy
Bellows Farm Inc.

Bellows Farm was more than a detox center for alcoholics. It also served as a training camp for elite athletes. In 1947 Murphy hosted two Finnish long-distance Olympian runners—Mikko Hietanen and Väinö Muinonen—while they prepared for the Boston Marathon. About twice a week they would have a steam bath at Bellows Farm and a massage by the longtime resident masseuse. Eddie the Rubber's skillful hands may have helped, as Hietanen placed second in the race.

Two years later, three brothers from Ireland—Shaun, Tim, and Patrick J. "Paddy" Regan—traveled to Murphy's farm to train before making their professional boxing debut in the United States. On April 4, 1949, the Regan brothers stepped off a plane at Logan Airport, where they were greeted by a crowd of boxing fans and popping flashbulbs. They were brought to Massachusetts by boxing promoter Sam Silverman and were nicknamed the "Mayo Brothers."

"If Regan's the name, why the Mayo moniker?" a man at the airport asked them.

"What better name for three fine lads from Ballyhaunis, County Mayo?" one of their handlers replied. "And besides, if you should happen to ask some of the fellers they tangled with, they'll tell ya—well, ya'll probably find them at the Mayo Clinic by now. Get what I mean?"

The three Irish boxers were whisked off to the State House, where they met Governor Paul Dever, who told them, "the best of luck, boys."

The boys seemed comfortable in the spotlight. "Everybody here seems Irish," said Tim Regan. "They should make Boston the capital of Ireland."

The brothers stayed the night at a hotel in Cambridge. They woke up to a breakfast of oatmeal, Irish bacon, and tea hosted by Cambridge Mayor Michael Neville and City Councilor Edward A. Crane. Then the Regans went off to Acton, so they could train at Dropkick Murphy's.

When they arrived at Bellows Farm, they walked into the gymnasium and marveled at the state-of-the-art equipment and regulation-size boxing ring. The brothers kicked off their shoes, scampered out onto the gleaming gymnasium floor, and began playing a spirited game of handball.

Later, Murphy took the boys out and got them their first ice cream soda. They looked puzzled by the straws sticking out of the ice cream. They preferred to use spoons instead. As they ate ice cream by the spoonsful and chugged Cokes and orange sodas, they took in the sounds of American pop songs playing on the jukebox, enjoying every moment of relaxation before they began training for their first professional bouts in the United States.

On April 18, 1949, marathon runner Johnny Kelley stopped by Bellows Farm for a visit. A photographer snapped a photo of Kelley running alongside the Regan brothers at the entrance to Bellows Farm.

Kelley ran the Boston Marathon sixty-one times. He took first place twice, once in 1935 and again in 1945. After his second finish, Kelley, who was then thirty-seven years old, said something that would have made Murphy and other fellow Actonians smile. When asked about the victory and the secret of his success, this was his response: "It's the air in Acton," he said. "A Finn up that way says it's the best air in the country. That's why so many Finns live in that section."

The summer of 1949 was a busy time in Dropkick's gym. In June 1949 the Lowell *Sun* reported that besides the Regan brothers, heavyweight Clyde Steeves was working out at Bellows Farm, as was featherweight Buddy Hayes. On June 22, middleweight Charlie Fusari was scheduled to train there. On July 6, Rocky Graziano was slated to arrive—the legendary middleweight had a match scheduled in West Springfield on July 18. (Years later, Graziano's life story was made into the Oscar-winning film *Somebody Up There Likes Me*, starring Paul Newman.)

Dropkick Murphy enjoyed having company over and welcomed anyone who wanted to watch the athletes train.

In 1951, "Dynamite" Joe Rindone trained at Bellows Farm for his match against "Irish" Bob Murphy at Braves Field. His trainer told the press that he brought Rindone to Acton to get him away from the city heat and off the corners of Roxbury at night. Rindone spent his days doing roadwork in Acton and Concord and boxing six rounds a day in preparation for his fight at Braves Field. Dropkick Murphy called it a "blood money" battle. "Boxing is a rough game," said Murphy, who pointed out that many fighters "get their brains scrambled without making any money."

Rindone had a chance to make between $17,000 and $20,000, Murphy said. "If he gets past [Bob] Murphy, he's set for the big dough. And he still has his senses."

Pro wrestlers also made frequent appearances at Bellows Farm. Gorgeous George visited Bellows Farm once and handed out gold bobby pins to the children. Dropkick Murphy's son David recalls playing pool with Gorgeous George and running an errand for him, taking his elaborately decorated wrestling robes to a stitching shop in the neighboring town of Maynard to be repaired. To this day, he remembers the weight of Gorgeous George's robes. "They were heavy," recalled David.

Dropkick Murphy was, by nature, a friendly, outgoing, hospitable guy. He enjoyed talking with people and spent lots of time on the phone chatting with folks. He welcomed sports fans into the gym at Bellows Farm to watch boxers train in the ring, and he never charged admission.

The Murphy children grew accustomed to meeting celebrities. Murphy's son, John, recalled that his father knew Joe DiMaggio: "Once in New York, I was on the street with my father when Joe DiMaggio came hustling out of a restaurant or bar. He nodded to my father and said, 'hi Murph.' That was a great moment for me."

10

THE FIGHTERS

You fight for your life
Because the fighter never quits
—"The Warrior's Code" by the Dropkick Murphys

O ne cold day in January 1953, a *Boston Globe* sportswriter named Herb Ralby strolled into a car dealership in Cambridge. Herb was a newspaper veteran, with almost twenty years of experience. He knew everyone in Boston's sports world, especially in the realms of hockey, boxing, and horse racing. He dressed sharply in bright colors. He wasn't there to buy an automobile, though. He was there to interview Tommy Collins, a local boxing phenom who was moonlighting as a car salesman.

Collins was twenty-three years old and selling cars to make some cash while his handlers arranged his next match. The blue-eyed boxer was from Dropkick's hometown of Medford and was considered the pride of Boston and beyond. He was handsome, with chiseled cheekbones and a square jaw, white teeth, a flashy smile, and an even flashier personality. A halo of charisma surrounded him.

Collins was a local boy made good. Born in the South End of Boston, he grew up one of sixteen children and shined shoes as a young boy. He only had an eighth-grade education, but he'd become a successful professional fighter and had moved to Medford. He was a spitfire both in and out of the ring, and although he weighed only 123 pounds, his lanky arms were deceivingly strong; the fighter could punch. He turned pro in November 1946 at age seventeen and had beaten many of the top featherweights in his division.

Ralby walked into the showroom and immediately spotted Collins, who was dressed in a gray flannel suit. Collins was clean-shaven, with his hair neatly combed. He turned around and saw Ralby, his big eyes lit up, and he greeted the reporter with a huge smile. Collins wasn't ashamed of his job at the car dealership. He needed money to live on between fights.

"My fight paydays are good, but they aren't often enough," Collins told the reporter. Collins also wanted to start saving the money he made from boxing because he had a family to support. And he knew his career wouldn't last forever.

"How much longer do you think you'll fight?" Ralby asked.

"A year, maybe two," said Collins. "My wife wants me to quit, but not right away. I think I can fight maybe two years, but if some twenty-one-year-old kid chases me out of the building some night as I've done to guys I've fought, I'll quit right then."

Ralby asked about Jimmy Carter, the lightweight boxing champion of the world.

"He'd have to weigh 135 pounds, and no more," said Collins. "I think I could beat him, too."

Ralby asked Collins about his previous slugfests and the punches he'd taken in the past. What if he takes too many to the head?

Collins said he wasn't worried about that. "My wife is a registered nurse," he said. "She knows enough about the body to recognize whether I'm slowing down or getting forgetful or something. If she ever does, I'm through. I hope though, she'll never have to tell me. I hope I know when to quit."

Collins had met his wife while nursing a rib injury at Boston City Hospital. His friends called the injury a "blessing in disguise" because he met his wife and she nursed him back to health. They had a child, Tommy Jr., who was now seven months old.

The last fight Collins had was with Lauro Salas of Mexico on December 8. That match was held at the Boston Garden before a sellout crowd, and Collins went down twice in the first round. But he ultimately emerged as the winner by unanimous decision. He and his wife had just moved into a new home. That was keeping him busy.

"Lots of curtains to hang, cleaning to be done, and furniture to be moved," he said.

"Can I sell you a car, Herb? This car has everything. Now this here model . . ."

That interview and subsequent story in the *Boston Globe* led up to an eventual announcement that Collins would face Carter in the ring for the championship title. The match was scheduled for April 24, 1953, at Boston Garden. To prepare for the fight, Collins was going to train at Bellows Farm.

In the weeks leading up to the fight, boxing fans and sportswriters began comparing the merits of the two pugilists. Outside the ring, Collins was outgoing and energetic and exuded confidence. He enjoyed hamming it up for the media and had no problem bragging about his accomplishments.

The champion, Jimmy Carter, was the opposite of Collins. Born in South Carolina and raised in Harlem, he was five years older than Collins and two inches shorter. Unlike Collins, who had a thin, lanky build, Carter was built like a fire hydrant—compact, sturdy, with thick legs, a broad chest, and strong shoulders. Carter was cool and calm, quiet and reserved. "Jimmy never gets excited," said his manager, Willie Ketchum. "He'll never lose a fight by blowing his stack."

In late March, Collins was working out at Stonehill College in Easton. But his manager, Rip Valenti, told him a change of venue was needed to prepare for the fight. He arranged for Collins to stay over and work out at Bellows Farm. "Dropkick has a better gym," said Valenti.

While speculation swirled around the upcoming fight, Collins said goodbye to his young wife and son and headed to Acton to train at Bellows Farm. He showed up at Dropkick Murphy's weighing 138 pounds and immediately started fight preparations under the direction of his trainer, Coogie McFarland.

Collins had a routine at Bellows Farm. He woke up at seven o'clock in the morning and started his day running along the rolling country roads of Acton. He'd jog for miles, past trees and shrubs and pastures, and when he returned, he'd relax and read the newspaper before eating breakfast. At around 1:30 in the afternoon, he began his hard workout in the gym. After his warm-up, he'd start punching the dark, teardrop-shaped speed bag dangling from a circular platform above his head. His fists moved fast, like a tornado, and the chain rattled as the bag hit the board over and over again. Then he moved on to the heavy bag, throwing punches at the big, stuffed cylinder hanging from the ceiling. Each punch landed with a dull thump.

✻ ✻ ✻

On April 9, 1953, groups of men filed into Dropkick Murphy's gym to watch Collins box. The fighter went six rounds, working with a rotating cast of three sparring partners, Rocky Sullivan, a former Golden Gloves boxer from Dorchester; Billy "Willie" Mays, an African American boxer from Roxbury; and Georgie Edmonds, a Jimmy Carter look-alike from Hartford, Connecticut. A cadre of men—nearly two hundred them—had gathered in Murphy's gym to watch the young dynamo practice as he prepared for his title bout.

When Collins finished, they clapped their hands. The applause didn't stop until Collins raised one of his gloved hands to quiet the room. This simple gesture hushed the chattering men. "Thank you, thank you," Collins said, addressing his little legion of fans. "All you fine people *should* feel happy. You know why? You saw six rounds of boxing—and at the Garden April 24 you'll only see one!"

The crowd roared with laughter. Tommy's eyes sparkled. He raised his arm again.

"I heard no hand, for my sparring partners."

Everyone clapped.

The next day, a smaller crowd congregated inside the gym to watch Collins in action. Outside, the weather was rainy and gray. When his trainers advised him to protect his chin and not take any stupid chances, Collins dismissed their advice.

"What's everybody worried about? I'll flatten him for sure," replied Collins, coolly.

Murphy walked into the room and asked the young protege what he wanted to eat. "Half a cow or a dozen pork chops or both?" chuckled Murphy. "We want to make sure you're absolutely physically fit and ready for this tough assignment."

Meanwhile, Jimmy Carter arrived in town. Carter acknowledged that he'd been reading about Collins and got a kick out of his boasting and what he'd been saying in the papers. When asked about the fight, Carter declined to make any predictions. His fists would do the talking.

That evening Collins went into Boston to accept an award at a special banquet dinner hosted by the Boston Sports Lodge of B'nai B'rith. The ceremony was held at the Sheraton Plaza hotel in Copley Square and over seven hundred people attended. Other honorees included Boston Celtics point guard Bob Cousy, Boston Red Sox center fielder Dom DiMaggio, Boston Bruins captain Milt Schmidt, sportswriter Dave Egan, and others. His rival, Jimmy Carter, presented him with the award. Upon accepting the honor, Collins smiled at the crowd and said, "I hope Carter is as generous with the lightweight title as he was with this plaque."

On April 21, 1953, a mother from the neighboring town of Maynard ushered her eight-year-old son into Collins's dressing room at Dropkick Murphy's. The little boy looked up shyly at the fighter, wide-eyed and slightly intimidated.

"He prays for you every night," said the mother, with a proud smile. "His older brother brought him into your dressing room the night you beat Salas. All he could see was your feet. But you've been his hero ever since."

Tommy beamed.

"Prays for me every night, does he? We'll take care of him good." Tommy turned to Coogie McFarland, his handler. "Coogie, get me a pair of trunks. This boy hasta have a pair of trunks."

McFarland handed him a green pair. Tommy promptly presented them to the boy.

An old veteran boxer watched the scene unfold and shook his head, smiling. "Only three days before the fight and this kid is entertaining in his room. Must be nuts. Old-timers wouldn't see anybody the week of a fight."

Collins was getting antsy. And slightly homesick. "Getting fed up," he said. "Wish it was Friday night and I was going into the ring. The clock don't turn very fast when you want something to happen."

Four pint-sized baseball players in Acton Little League uniforms bounded into the room. They had cards in their hands. Collins sat down, thanked the boys, and autographed each one.

"Don't forget to say a prayer for me, fella," he said, handing the signed cards back to the boys.

Collins didn't mind taking a break from the limelight now and again. Occasionally he would take the time in between training sessions to go to Lowell to watch a movie. With a five o'clock shadow, wearing a pork-pie fedora, he'd settle into a seat at the darkened theater, stare at the big screen before him, and try to take his mind off everything for an hour or two.

And when the sun set over Acton, and Collins lay in bed trying to block out the sound of Coogie, perhaps he imagined he was back home, holding his baby with his wife Mae lying beside him.

Though Collins longed for home, all around him, anticipation was building.

The whole city was rooting for Collins, the spunky underdog. "This is Boston's most important bout ever, with the most at stake, the biggest gate, the heaviest gambling, and the largest audience," wrote Harold Kaese on the front page of the *Boston Globe* on April 24.

Unlike Collins, Carter didn't boast. He looked calm and relaxed before the big match. When asked to share his thoughts on the outcome of the fight, Carter politely declined. "I never make predictions," he said.

For Collins, it was the biggest fight of his career. A crowd of 12,477 attended the match at Boston Garden, and TV viewers across the country settled into their seats to watch Collins take on Carter, the lightweight champion of the world.

Collins entered the ring like a jumping jack, bursting with energy and enthusiastically punching the air as he jumped around the ring. From the ringside seats all the way up to the rafters of the Boston Garden, fans cheered and whistled. While Collins bounced around wildly, Carter entered the ring slowly, his demeanor reserved.

In Collins's corner were Johnny Conlon, John Clinton, and Coogie McFarland. In Carter's corner were his manager Willie Ketchum, Sam Cherin, and Chickie Ferrara. The referee was Tommy Rawson, an old-school, blue-eyed boxer from East Boston.

The fight got underway. Collins's face absorbed a left punch from Carter. Then Collins landed a right to Carter's jaw.

Collins's wife, Mae, did not see this. She was at home, kneeling on the floor. She closed her eyes and breathed heavily, trying to imagine how he was doing. She refused to look at the television.

Carter dominated the fight from the start, but Collins hung tough.

In the third round, Carter landed a strong left hook and Collins appeared stunned by the blow. But Collins kept going and fought back with a flurry of sloppy punches. Carter defended himself easily and pushed Collins away. Carter then stepped in and was about to throw another punch when suddenly, almost without warning, Collins dropped to the canvas. Carter looked genuinely surprised as he watched Collins topple backward. Collins hit the canvas so hard that his legs and feet bounced up upon impact.

Rawson began counting. "One, two, three . . ." Collins was on his back, his arms over his head. Flashbulbs went off. He blinked his eyes and held onto the middle rope as he slowly got back up.

Once he was on his feet, Collins marched right back toward Carter. Carter began unloading punches, and Collins appeared incapable of defending himself. Carter threw a hard right, and then another. Collins went down again. And once again he got back up, refusing to surrender.

Carter continued to pummel Collins with punches, knocking him down again and again. When Collins rose to his feet, he swung wildly at the air. Carter didn't seem to exert much effort as he landed shots to Collins's head.

Millions of viewers sitting in their living rooms across the country watched in horror. Children were ordered out of parlors so as not to witness the violence being broadcast on television. At the Gillette Safety Razor Company in South Boston, the match was broadcast for employees. Eighty-nine television sets at the Gillette plant were broadcasting the match for 2,600 employees and their guests, who were cheering Collins on during the first round.

"Let's go, Tommy!"

"Finish him quick, Tom!"

By the second round, their optimistic cheers had turned to groans. Before the third round was over, Collins had hit the canvas seven times. A sense of desperation fell over the audience at Gillette as they stood by helplessly and watched Collins get pummeled.

In the ring, Collins moved sluggishly. The bright lights shined off his forehead and revealed a cut over his eye. One of his eyes was completely swollen shut. But Collins once again rose from the canvas, standing up and teetering before he regained his balance. He pushed away from the referee and nodded that he was okay.

Each time, Rawson, the referee, wiped off Collins's gloves on his shirt and yelled into his ear, asking if he was all right.

Collins yelled back that he was.

Carter's manager, Willie Ketchum, was concerned and tried to get Rawson's attention. He looked at him and said, "What do you want to do, get him killed?"

At the end of the third round, Collins wandered to the wrong corner. He put his fists up and shadowboxed an invisible opponent until his cornermen rushed over and guided him toward his corner.

At the start of the fourth round, Carter and Collins exchanged punches. Collins just missed being hit by a left. For a brief moment, it looked like an even fight. Collins had escaped, perhaps he could do it again. But then Carter cracked Collins with a right, and Collins dropped to the canvas like a cadaver. The camera bulbs flashed, reflecting off Collins's pale arms and ribs. He got up again, only to be hit in the jaw and sent to the floor. He got up again, but Carter again knocked him down. It was still only the fourth round.

Rawson, the referee, knelt beside Collins and began counting. He didn't get past six. Collins's handlers were now in the ring. Rawson was forced to end the contest and waved to Carter's corner, signaling that the fight was over.

After the fight, Collins stretched out on a long table in his dressing room at Boston Garden. His right eye socket and cheekbone were shiny and bulbous, his eyelids swollen shut. His manager, Johnny Conlon, knelt by his side, holding his right hand. "I couldn't get started," Collins said. "I don't know what hit me."

The following day, newspaper headlines read: "One of Most Brutal Fights Ever" and "Capital Punishment Next on TV?" The *New York Times* called it "one of the most reprehensible mismatches in modern ring history." *Time* magazine called it the "Boston Massacre" and said that TV viewers "got more violence than they could stomach."

Dave Egan of the Boston *Daily Record* castigated the referee and wrote that Rawson "permitted this boy to take a beating that would have started a street fight had it been administered to a dog or horse."

Boston City Councilor Frederick C. Hailer Jr. called the match "a show of barbarism."

"To let a boy with Collins's courage almost get killed isn't the right sort of boxing," he said. "The boxing commission should be made to answer for this. It could have been a tragedy."

Robert K. Christenberry, chairman of the New York State Athletic Commission, watched the fight on television and called it "disgraceful" and detrimental to the sport of boxing. "Where were the doctors? Why didn't they stop it quicker?" Christenberry asked. "Everything we've done to make it a clean, competitive sport they've thrown to the wind."

Christenberry said Collins should have only been given three or at most maybe four knockdowns. He would later describe the controversial fight as "probably the most deplorable thing I've ever seen."

"Millions of people witnessed this black eye to boxing," Christenberry said, "and it will take a long time for boxing to make up for it."

Jimmy Carter said the fight "turned my stomach," and he considered asking the referee to end it, but he didn't think Rawson would listen. "They shouldn't have asked him to come out there again," Carter said. "The referee should have stopped it."

Carter's manager, Willie Ketchum, also thought the fight should have ended earlier. "Rawson should have stepped in after Collins was knocked down seven times in the third round. Collins has guts enough for ten fighters."

After the fight, Collins hit the showers. It didn't take long before he was joking with reporters. "I feel fine. Haven't got an ache in my body," he said. "Don't I look OK?"

Collins said he supported Rawson's decision to keep the fight going. "I was still swinging, wasn't I?" Collins said. "It was for the world championship, why should he stop it?"

Rawson called Collins at home. Collins answered: "Hello, pal. I ought to hit you with a baseball bat for stopping the fight."

"Was I wrong, Tommy?"

Collins put up his fists. "I got only one beef, you stopped it too soon," said Collins with a grin.

But Collins's good humor and cheerful disposition didn't ease the minds of those who witnessed the slugfest. One *New York Mirror* writer described it as "boxing in its most sadistic form," while the *Chicago Tribune* called it "one of the most revolting spectacles ever presented under the name of sport."

The governor of Massachusetts, Christian A. Herter, called for a special meeting of the state boxing commission to discuss the fight.

Massachusetts Boxing Commissioner Henry Lamar was a strong advocate for instituting a "three-knockdown rule," which meant that any boxer who got floored three times in the same round would be declared knocked out and the fight would be over. Such a rule, Lamar said, would "protect every boxer."

The referee, Tommy Rawson, was ultimately cleared of wrongdoing, but the brutal match had a lasting effect on the sport, as several states adopted the three-knockdown rule.

The *New York Times* would later report: "The savagery of the beating helped to create the three-knockdown rule almost universally in effect now; when a fighter is knocked down three times, the bout is ended."

At the end of June 1954, Tony DeMarco, a talented Italian kid from the North End of Boston, came out to start training at Dropkick Murphy's facility to prepare for his next bout. It was going to be a big one for him, held at Fenway Park. His opponent was George Araujo, a boxer from Rhode Island. They were close in age (Araujo had just turned twenty-three) and both sons of immigrants (Araujo's father was originally from the Cape Verde islands).

DeMarco's real name was Leonard Liotta, and everyone called him "Nardo." His parents came from Sicily, his father worked as a cobbler, and he was raised on Fleet Street in Boston's Little Italy, the North End, not far from Boston Garden. As a youngster, Nardo worked as a shoeshine boy and delivered newspapers. When he first started boxing, he wasn't old enough to compete legally. But that didn't get in the way of launching his boxing career. He convinced his older friend Tony to let him use his name and his baptismal certificate (as proof of his age) so he could get his amateur boxing license. From that point on, he boxed as Tony DeMarco.

DeMarco was naturally a southpaw but learned to box orthodox and ended up developing a deadly left hook. He was a slugger and a dogged competitor who fought aggressively and wore his opponents down over the course of a fight.

DeMarco followed a typical boxer's workout regimen at Bellows Farm. He jumped rope, hit the speed bag, sparred with partners in the ring, and ran outside along the dirt roads in Acton.

Tommy Collins was also training at Bellows Farm, preparing for his comeback. In addition to sparring and doing roadwork, Murphy provided them with an axe so they could chop wood.

Collins hadn't fought in over a year. But the anticipation was building. Again.

"I have to find out once and for all if I can still fight," said Collins. "It's better to find out now than in another five years. I just got to get it out of my system."

DeMarco agreed to slim down to 142 and a half pounds for the fight. He had a lot of training to do, and since he moved into a room at Bellows Farm, he didn't need his car. One morning he got back from a long run and got a surprise when he sat down to read the paper at breakfast. There was his name, on the front page.

No. End Gang Beats Korea Vet in Revere
Flee in Car Owned by Boxer DeMarco

DeMarco had let a friend borrow his 1954 Chevy Bel Air while he was away. It turned out his pal got into a brawl with some guys at Revere Beach, and when they left, the police traced the license plate back to DeMarco. The police showed up at his family's home in the North End, and his sister explained that her brother was out of town preparing for the big fight. DeMarco's friend went to the police and explained what happened, then drove DeMarco's car out to Dropkick Murphy's and handed the keys over to DeMarco. "I was pretty ticked off at him," DeMarco recalled in his 2011 autobiography, *Nardo: Memoirs of a Boxing Champion*.

By July 6, DeMarco was doing everything he could to drop weight. On this hot summer day, he wore two T-shirts, two pairs of trunks, and heavy socks made of wool. DeMarco blamed his extra pounds on good old-fashioned Italian home cooking.

"I was down to 141 last Friday night, so I called it quits Saturday and Sunday," DeMarco said. "I went home and ate. That Italian food put me back to where I am today." No one in DeMarco's camp would reveal how many pounds he had to lose, but observers guessed it had to be five or six.

DeMarco and Araujo were supposed to weigh in at 2 p.m. for their July 12 fight. If DeMarco didn't weigh in at 142 and a half pounds, he'd have to pay a hefty forfeit fee to his opponent.

DeMarco wasn't just training his body; he was training his mind as well. Under the tutelage of trainer Sammy Fuller, he was learning new strategies and developing new habits.

On the morning of Sunday, July 11, Tony DeMarco and Tommy Collins attended the seven o'clock mass at Our Lady Help of Christians Church in West Concord. The local newspaper noted that DeMarco took communion on the day before he fought Araujo at Fenway. It would be his toughest opponent yet.

On July 12, 1954, the night of the big fight, DeMarco met Araujo under the lights at Fenway Park, surrounded by a crowd of about ten thousand. DeMarco came out strong in the first round, but the nimble Araujo held on in the second and third rounds, dodging DeMarco's powerful hooks and landing jabs whenever he could.

At the end of the fourth round, DeMarco went to his corner. Fuller looked at DeMarco and told him what he needed to do. "He's standing up straight and trying to box," said Fuller. "Go in low, jab to the body, and throw the overhand right to the head, just like we practiced at Dropkick's."

DeMarco did just that. As Araujo tried to get a shot in, DeMarco suddenly blasted him with a powerful right. Araujo went down and came back up only to be crushed by DeMarco's combination punches to his head and body. The fifth round ended up being the last. DeMarco was declared the victor by a technical knockout.

After the fight, DeMarco said the insight he gained at Bellows Farm had helped him win. "When I saw him throw that left lead, I remembered something they told me at camp [at Dropkick Murphy's in Acton]," he said. "They said to hold him off a little with my own left and slam the right over. I did and it worked."

Tommy Collins made his comeback on August 12, 1954, at the Boston Arena. The training that he put in at Bellows Farm paid off when he met his opponent, Jimmy Ithia of New York. They went four rounds. In the third, Ithia began to fade, and Collins landed a few hooks to his body. In the fourth round, Collins got Ithia on the chin. Ithia went down and the referee counted ten. Collins won by a knockout.

Collins went on to win his next two matches at Boston Arena.

The most important victory for DeMarco would come the following year, in April 1955, when he took on Johnny Saxton for the welterweight title at Boston Garden.

Saxton was managed by Frank "Blinky" Palermo, an organized crime associate of Frankie Carbo, the underworld "Czar of Boxing." ("Wiseguys were part of boxing," recalled DeMarco. "That's how it was in those days.")

DeMarco was the underdog. At the start of the fight, the odds were 100–35 in Saxton's favor. But those placing bets—including Saxton's mob-connected handlers—underestimated DeMarco.

It was a battle, and by the ninth round, it was still close. When DeMarco hit Saxton on the chin in the fourteenth round, Saxton toppled backward onto the ropes. He went down but slowly got back up on his feet. Then DeMarco trapped Saxton in the corner and started pummeling him, throwing punches continuously. Saxton appeared to be stunned and stood there, defenseless. After DeMarco landed twenty-four unanswered punches in a row, the referee stopped the match.

DeMarco was crowned welterweight champion of the world. His whole neighborhood celebrated his victory. One of their own had made it to the big time. Italian residents of the North End shoved up their windows and screamed out to the streets in their native tongue, "Campione del mondo!"

Dave Egan nicknamed him "The Flame and Fury of Fleet Street."

Many decades later, Tony DeMarco recalled fond memories of training at Dropkick Murphy's. "It was a very nice place, very well kept," said DeMarco. For a city kid, "it was different." Acton was definitely more convenient and closer to home. "That was a good spot. It was close by. I enjoyed it."

11

GHOSTS OF BELLOWS FARM

*And how would you like to be Joe Kennedy? Here's your uncle,
looking more like an escapee from Dropkick Murphy's every day,
and he says he's going to run again in 1994?*
—Howie Carr, October 28, 1991

Sometime after 1:15 a.m. on November 5, 1957, a custodian at Bellows Farm was making his rounds when he noticed flames in the dormitory. He immediately ran over to the intercom system and shouted, "Help, fire, fire!"

Murphy's second oldest son, David, was seventeen at the time. He recalls that his younger brother Johnny, who was about nine years old, had adopted a little stray mutt named Ace. The dog had already been barking. "The dog woke everybody up," said David. That was their first alert that something was wrong.

"My father and me went up there, to the first bungalow," said David. "It was engulfed."

Flames spread quickly through the nine-room dormitory. The gym, maintenance building, and staff housing at Bellows Farm were also on fire. The smoke was so thick, "you couldn't see inside the windows," recalled David.

"My father broke the window, and out poured heavy black smoke," he said.

Dropkick Murphy dove through the window and placed his hands on a nearby bed, trying to feel if anyone was there. David said his father must have been holding his breath because he did this silently. Meanwhile, David waited outside anxiously, waiting for his father.

"I was hoping he would come out," said David.

The Acton Fire Department sent seven trucks, sirens clanging, to Davis Road. Fire Chief H. Stuart MacGregor sounded a general alarm, and trucks from Maynard, Concord, and Littleton came to help. The firefighters had to haul hose lines from Route 2A because there were no hydrants close by—the nearest one was a quarter mile away.

With the help of the firemen, Dropkick Murphy tried to evacuate as many patients as he could. But they couldn't get to everyone. Upstairs in his bedroom on the second floor was Reinert J. Anderson, the sixty-eight-year-old resident dishwasher of Bellows Farm. Anderson woke up to find himself surrounded in thick smoke. Coughing and gasping, he tried to get out of bed but never made it to the door. He passed out and died in his bedroom.

John Quigley, a sixty-six-year-old insurance broker from the nearby town of Arlington, also found himself trapped in the burning building. He was patient at Bellows Farm and tried to escape, but he must have lost his way. His badly burned body wasn't found until the following morning in the rear building.

Six others were injured in the blaze. Two patients were overcome by smoke and had to be taken to Emerson Hospital. Murphy burned his hand while trying to rescue guests. He wrapped it in a bandage.

A nine-room dormitory, known as the "bungalow," the gym, the maintenance building, and a two-and-a-half-story employee dorm were all connected and destroyed in the blaze. The local newspaper called it the worst fire in Acton's history.

Murphy wrote a note of thanks that was printed on the front page of the Acton *Beacon* on November 14, 1957:

I wish to express my gratitude to the Acton Fire Department and other local fire departments who aided them in extinguishing the fire at Bellows Farms Sanitarium on November 5, 1957. Their prompt response and able performance of their duties prevented much greater damage. I also wish to thank our neighbors and friends in Acton who so generously offered their assistance during a difficult time.

Sincerely,
John E. Murphy

The fire was followed by another family tragedy. After several months of being ill, Dropkick Murphy's wife, Marie, died in a Boston hospital in March 1958. She was just forty-five years old. John Murphy suddenly found himself a single father to his three sons, Richard, David, and John.

Much changed in the years that followed. Dropkick Murphy later married Marie's sister, Jean. They would have four more children: Michael, Marie, Susan, and Amy.

Murphy continued to operate Bellows Farm until 1971, when he decided to close the sanitarium for good. After it shut down, several of his regular patients started going to Valleyhead Hospital in Carlisle to dry out until it closed in 1978.

When he reflected on his career at Bellows Farm, he wondered how his patients fared. Maybe, just maybe, some of them chose to stay sober.

"Maybe it was a dead-end for some, I don't know. Maybe some of them left here and never drank again. This place is pretty and healthful and everything like that," said Murphy, "but booze is a terrible equalizer."

He continued: "They were not all hopeless. I don't think any of them were hopeless, just a lot of men sick and tired of being sick and tired."

When Bellows Farm closed, the *Boston Herald Traveler* estimated that Dropkick Murphy had been a "mother hen to a parade of forty thousand alcoholics" since he'd opened his sanitarium. Considering how many years he devoted to helping alcoholics, Murphy may have helped more people battle addiction than any other pro athlete in American sports history at the time.

After Murphy stopped admitting patients, the sign for Bellows Farm was taken down, and the country estate that was once known as Bellows Farm began to change. Land was divided into lots and homes were built. Some of the property was set aside as conservation land. Murphy turned his focus to managing his real estate.

Acton had seen a huge growth spurt. In 1950 the population was 3,500; by 1970 it had grown to nearly 15,000. As the years went by, and more new people moved into town, Bellows Farm became a distant memory. What was once a well-known landmark in Acton gradually became a piece of forgotten history.

Dropkick Murphy died on October 17, 1977.

On February 28, 2006, the Dropkick Murphys appeared on *Late Night with Conan O'Brien* and performed a song from their fifth studio album, "The Warrior's Code." The title of the song was "Sunshine Highway," and the lyrics were inspired by Dropkick Murphy's detox center at Bellows Farm.

> *Yeah me and my girl we're acting up again all right*
> *She ain't much of a looker, she can handle her Paraldehyde . . .*

That's how the song starts. And it continues:

> *Take another ride on the sunshine highway*
> *Take another ride try to turn it around*
> *Take another ride down the sunshine highway*
> *Take another ride try to turn it around tonight*

> *Drop me off, sign me in, clean me up and let me out*
> *Man that nurse is a bitch, this sucks, she says my jug ain't allowed . . .*

Ken Casey said the concept for the song came from someone who was a patient at Bellows Farm. An older man told them that the road leading into Dropkick Murphy's was known as the "Sunshine Highway" because of how it looked at night. He said the asphalt was covered with bits of broken glass bottles that sparkled and glistened in the darkness.

"They called it the Sunshine Highway because when the headlights hit it, it was all broken glass from people taking their last drink on the way in and throwing it out the window," said Casey. "The road would light up."

"That whole story is about one gentleman's recollection of the place, that whole song actually. It's funny because, a couple of people, when that song came out, we never thought twice, but they were like, 'What do you mean, Sunshine Highway?' They thought it was about going to Florida or something," Casey laughed. "It's definitely not about going to Florida."

Decades before the Betty Ford Center opened its doors—and long before the band Dropkick Murphys named themselves in his honor—Dr. John

"Dropkick" Murphy dedicated himself to helping people struggling with alcoholism. His rural retreat became a symbol of hope for alcoholics and their families.

Few traces of Bellows Farm remain today, but they are there if you know where to look. The big red barn that served as the headquarters for Dropkick Murphy's operation still stands. It's now an office building that houses several local businesses, including a law office, a physician's office, and a French-language school. But most people who enter the big red barn have no idea that it was once home to one of the most famous detox centers around.

In some respects Bellows Farm was an early forerunner to celebrity detox centers of today. But what made Dropkick Murphy's sanitarium unique is that it wasn't just a detox center—it was also a top-notch training facility for elite athletes and a public gym that offered supervised weight-lifting and fitness sessions to average folks who wanted to get in shape.

It was this interesting setup that made Bellows Farm stand out and created an atmosphere where alcoholic patients didn't have to undergo detox in isolation. At Bellows Farm, they were able to dry out in the presence of athletes, visitors, and members of Dropkick Murphy's own family.

There typically wasn't much interaction between the athletes and the alcoholics at Bellows Farm, except when patients would occasionally go inside the gym and watch boxers work out and spar in the ring. But having the gym there, and having pro athletes visit the property so often, perhaps provided inspiration to some patients at Bellows Farm. It's also possible that the patients taught the athletes something, too, about the dangers of addiction and alcohol abuse, and its ability to ravage the mind, body, and soul.

One thing is for sure: Murphy's sports-centric approach to health and wellness drew many followers, and perhaps there are lessons that can be learned from him today.

And his legend continues to live on.

EPILOGUE

Bobby Byrne ended up staying sober and opened his own bar on Cape Cod.

Jimmy Carter became the first boxer to win the world lightweight title three times. He retired from the ring in 1960 and was later inducted into the International Boxing Hall of Fame.

Tommy Collins would make a comeback, losing his next match in June 1953 and then winning the next three. But his fight against Lulu Perez in December 1954 was his last. He lost and retired from boxing for good at the age of twenty-five. He then got a job working as a Middlesex Superior Court officer and taught youth boxing. Collins died in 1996.

Tony DeMarco died in October 2021. A statue of him stands at the corner of Hanover and Cross streets in Boston's North End and there's also a street named in his honor. He was inducted into the International Boxing Hall of Fame in 2019.

Gene Mack, the cartoonist who first made Dropkick Murphy famous, died in July 1953 at his home in Medford. When the high school gym was named after him, more than eight hundred people attended the dedication ceremony commemorating the artist known as "Medford's Number One Fan."

The Mechanics Building, where Dropkick Murphy wrestled in 1933, was demolished in 1959. It was replaced by the Prudential Center.

William Muldoon died in 1933. The barn in Belfast, New York, where he trained John L. Sullivan, is now home to the Bare Knuckle Boxing Hall of Fame.

Jean Murphy, Dropkick Murphy's second wife, died on August 24, 2016, at her home in Acton.

Richard "Dick" H. Murphy, Dropkick Murphy's oldest son, died in 2004 at the age of sixty-seven. The trails that he created along the Nashoba Brook can still be accessed by the public today.

Valley Arena, Holyoke's legendary sporting venue, caught on fire twice (once in 1943, and then again in 1952) and was rebuilt each time. A wrestling show (featuring a female wrestler taking on a 450-pound bear in the main event) on May 11, 1960, marked the end of an era, as a third fire destroyed the building the next day. The site is now a public park.

Winn Robbins had a long career with the Boston Fire Department and retired as a lieutenant of Engine 55 in West Roxbury. According to his obituary in the *Boston Globe*, Robbins realized his dream of playing the drums for the Boston Symphony Orchestra before he died in 1998 at the age of eighty-nine.

ACKNOWLEDGMENTS

When I first embarked on this project, I had no idea how difficult it would be to unearth details about a long-closed sanitarium. This book was the result of many years of research. I followed every paper trail I could. I corresponded with historians, professional wrestling experts, law enforcement officials, and the children of professional wrestlers who had long since passed away. I interviewed Murphy's family and former staff members who worked at Bellows Farm and had the great fortune of speaking with boxing champion Tony DeMarco, who trained at Dropkick Murphy's gym in the 1950s, and Bobby Byrne, who had been a patient in the detox program and was kind enough to share his documents—and many memories—from his stay there.

I traveled to several different libraries and searched microfilm collections and databases for any mention of Dropkick and Bellows Farm. I dug into archives, studied old maps, reviewed census records, and read old newspaper accounts of wrestling matches and A.A. meetings.

I requested copies of marriage, birth, and death certificates. I called the church where Dropkick Murphy was baptized, contacted the schools he attended, and tracked down his high school yearbooks. I pored over countless books and watched grainy film footage of wrestling matches from the 1930s and '40s.

Most important of all, I met and spoke with Murphy's wife, Jean, his children, and other family members who graciously provided me with as much information as they could, time and time again. Without their cooperation, this book would not have been possible. I want to thank the Murphy family for being so generous with their time and allowing me to tell Dropkick's story, which turned out to be more amazing than I ever imagined.

I want to thank my agent, Matthew Valentinas of Kneerim & Williams, my publisher, Kyle Sarofeen of Hamilcar Publications, and copyeditor Shannon LeMay-Finn for making this book a reality. I tip my hat to Jay Manning and the rest of the crew at Crossroads for telling me about Bellows Farm and introducing me to the Murphy family. I'm grateful to Ken Casey, Brian Cook, Sam Ford, and Keith Wallman for their kind words of encouragement and support over the years. I appreciate all the people who took the time to share their expertise with me on a range of topics, including Robert Sabourin (firefighting); author Julian Shabazz (the experiences of black pro wrestlers); author William White (addiction and recovery); Leo Sullivan (public transportation); and Christine Lewis and the International Boxing Research Organization (health farms and boxing training camps). I also want to thank everyone who helped me track down photographs, video, documents, and other sources for the book, including Elizabeth Bouvier, the head of archives for the Massachusetts Supreme Judicial Court; DeSoto Brown of the Bishop Museum Archives; Scott George; Bill Klauer; Victoria Beyer from the Acton Historical Commission, the staff and volunteers at the Acton Public Library, the Albert R. and Mabel G. Jenks Library, and the Acton Historical Society.

Many of the people in this book were no longer living when I embarked on this project, and their surviving family members gave me insight into their lives and access to their personal documents and photos, including Whitey Kaunfer's son, Alvan Kaunfer; Kaimon Kudo's daughter, Mary Ann Kishiyama; Jerry Torti's (a.k.a. Jose Firpo) daughter, Dianne M. Impallaria; Dr. LeRoy P. Houck's son, Malcolm Houck; and of course, Dropkick Murphy's children.

Joe Opiela generously provided me with rare film footage of Dropkick Murphy in action, and Keith P. Chevalier and Laurie Morrissey kindly dug through Saint Anselm College's archives to find information on the school's football team from 1930.

I owe special thanks to Scott Teal of Crowbar Press for sharing his photos and knowledge of the world of professional wrestling, and a huge shout-out to Tim Hornbaker, Steven Johnson, Greg Oliver, Steve Yohe, the late J Michael Kenyon, and all the other professional wrestling historians who spent countless hours uncovering details that proved to be invaluable when I first started doing my own research into the history of the sport. I learned so much from them.

And last but not least I want to thank all my friends, family (Ma, Ed, Charlie, Julie, Eamon, Dad), my girlfriend Cody, and the teammates from my Shamrocks ice hockey team for putting up with me while I wrote this book.

ENDNOTES

Introduction

There were rumors that Dropkick Murphy's farm was a "secret hangout" where "businessmen, fire and police chiefs, politicians, and priests from New York and New England could go to relax and tie one on for a few days without worrying about political blowback," according to Joe Flood's book, *The Fires: How a Computer Formula, Big Ideas, and the Best of Intentions Burned Down New York City—and Determined the Future of Cities*. In the book, Flood makes a point to say that "it's notoriously hard to cull truth from rumor concerning Dropkick Murphy's," and he says there were also stories of it being a "brutal rehab facility where Boston's skid row winos were sent to dry out."

George V. Higgins paid homage to Dropkick Murphy in his 1974 novel, *Cogan's Trade*. But Higgins never mentioned where Murphy's sanitarium was located.

In Leigh Montville's 2004 biography of Ted Williams, Dropkick Murphy's farm was mistakenly identified as being located in Athol, an old mill town in central Massachusetts. Another book that got the location of Bellows Farm wrong was Professor Erwin H. Ford II's biography of George V. Higgins, which mistakenly placed Murphy's sanitarium in Fitchburg.

Chapter 1: All Saints' Eve

To write the description of a person getting dropkicked in the face, I studied photographs and film of Dropkick Murphy performing his signature move on various opponents. One thing that made Murphy stand out was his ability to jump up high enough to reach the other person's head and neck, and he could do this over and over again. Opponents of Murphy would jerk their necks back and contort their faces when they got kicked. Even when they were fully prepared to be kicked in the face, Murphy's boot often still made contact with their head, and I believe it's very likely that some felt the impact in the way I described.

The four quotes in italics are direct quotations of phrases uttered by wrestling fans during the time period that Murphy wrestled. "C'mon . . . fight 'im!" and "Kill 'im!" came from *The Revenge of Hatpin Mary: Women, Professional Wrestling and Fan Culture in the 1950s* by Chad Dell, pages 29 and 106; "How do you like that?" is a quote from an article titled "A Reporter at Large: Pull His Whiskers" by A. J. Liebling in the *New Yorker*, July 8, 1939; and the quote "Give it to him!" appeared in a wrestling story in the *New Castle* (Pennsylvania) *News* on June 26, 1936.

"Mechanics Hall"—I used many sources to describe the architecture of the Mechanics Hall, including photos from the Library of Congress and Historic American Buildings Survey; *King's Handbook of Boston* by Moses King (1881); *Some Prominent Buildings in the Newer Boston* (1903) by Frederick Pope; *Boston Illustrated: Containing Full Descriptions of the City and Its Immediate Suburbs, Its Public Buildings and Institutions, Business Edifices, Parks and Avenues, Statues, Harbor and Islands, Etc., Etc. with Numerous Historical Allusions* by Edward Stanwood, Houghton, Mifflin and Company (1886); and an excellent article from the *American Architect and Architecture*, Volume 9, J. R. Osgood & Company, 1881. Several articles from the *Boston Globe* were also helpful, including "Mechanics Gone, but Remembered," from February 21, 1965; "An Ugly Duckling Lives on for Many" from January 28, 1979; "Start to Tear Down Mechanics Bldg. Dec. 1" from October 25, 1958; and "Mechanics Part of Hub History" from January 9, 1959.

A list of events held at the Mechanics Hall can be found in various newspaper articles and an Associated Press article from April 15, 1958, titled "Historic Mechanics Building Doomed to Disappear from Boston Scene in a Few Years."

Charlie Gordon's real name was Charles Gordon Faux. His date of birth and eye color are listed on his World War I registration card. His naturalization petition shows that he had been born in England on May 5, 1889, and came to the United States as an infant in 1891.

The quote about Ted Germaine being a "master at arousing hate" came from the May 1, 1937, edition of the *Cambridge Sentinel*.

"One in five Bostonians was originally from the Emerald Isle"—This figure came from a report from April 1933 titled *Social Statistics by Census Tracts in Boston, Boston Council of Social Agencies*. An article in the *Boston Globe* on June 19, 1930 ('Twelve in 100 Foreign Born'), reported that 165,000 residents of Boston had been born in Ireland or had at least one parent who'd been born there. The population of Boston in 1930 was 781,188.

The quote "not too big to be slow, and large enough to be strong" appeared in the *Cambridge Sentinel* on August 11, 1934.

The reference to "thousands of Murphys listed in the city directory"—There were over 2,300 instances of the last name "Murphy" in the Boston city directory (Sampson & Murdock Co. 1925).

The reference to ten million gallons of beer sold came from a *Boston Globe* article titled "Six Months of Beer: Ten Million Gallons Sold in Massachusetts" by Henry Harris, October 15, 1933.

The descriptions of local Halloween festivities, pranks and mischief-making, and the costumes children were wearing were reported by the *Boston Globe* in a front-page story titled "Young and Old Mark Halloween" on November 1, 1933. I also gleaned information from articles and display advertisements that were published in the *Boston Herald*, *Boston Globe*, and *Boston Post* on and around October 31, 1933.

Advertisements for the Chateau Basque appeared in MIT's student newspaper, *The Tech*, on October 27, 1933, and Boston College's student newspaper, *The Heights*, on September 27 and October 25, 1933.

A detailed account of the hobo party at Simmons College and photos of the students' costumes were featured in the 1934 Simmons College yearbook.

Unemployment figures came from a January 16, 1933, *Boston Globe* article and two government reports titled *Social Statistics by Census Tracts in Boston* that were published in April 1933 and July 1935 by the Boston Council of Social Agencies.

"musty"—The Mechanics Building was described as a "dingy, musty, inconvenient old barn" in a letter to the editor that was published in the *Boston Globe* on November 1, 1950.

"popcorn"— "Sportsman's Show Offers Sterling Amusement for Discriminating Taste of Virile Bostonians," *Harvard Crimson*, February 7, 1935.

"Shared a dressing room"—Lou Thesz's autobiography *Hooker* describes in detail wrestling dressing rooms from that era.

"Essex coupes"—By 1929, Essex was the third-best-selling car in the country, according to *Popular Mechanics*. Chrysler, Ford, and Chevrolet were the three biggest carmakers in the United States in the early 1930s, according to *Riding the Roller Coaster: A History of the Chrysler Corporation*, by Charles K. Hyde.

The gray fedora was the most popular hat style in Boston at the time, according to an October 15, 1933, *Boston Globe* article by Joseph Dineen.

I mentioned that the "moon loomed large" and "moonlight poured through" windows because a *Boston Globe* article from November 1, 1933, stated that there was "a full moon hovering over the city" on Halloween night. Lunar calendars from 1933 show that it was indeed close to being a full moon (the true full moon actually occurred two days later, on November 2, 1933).

"the clerestory windows"—These are described in the article titled "Details of the Massachusetts Charitable Mechanic Association's Building" from an 1881 edition of *American Architect and Architecture.*

"Hello! Hello! Hello!"—This was Whitey Kaunfer's trademark opening line and is cited in many newspaper articles. In a letter to the editor dated April 18, 1999, retired *Globe* writer William Buchanan recalled how Kaunfer used to announce Charlie Gordon's midweek matches at the Mechanics Building. In a *Globe* article from November 7, 1973, Buchanan wrote that Kaunfer worked at Dropkick Murphy's matches at the Mechanics Building.

"Tell Charlie (Gordon), it looks like 35"—This quote came from an article by William Buchanan titled "With Harry Kaunfer at Ringside, It Was Always Hello, Hello, Hello," which ran in the *Boston Globe* on April 12, 1981.

"on the card that night"—Story about the bouts that night appeared in the November 1, 1933, *Boston Globe* article titled "Mephisto Flattens Germaine by Punch."

"How the hell are ya?"—This quote appeared in an article titled "Chuckles in Sports World: Humorous Tales Anent Announcers' Mike Slips Start Gales of Laughter" by Harold Kaese, *Boston Globe*, February 13, 1946.

The description of Whitey glancing around the auditorium, calculating attendance, putting his hat on the microphone, and his other mannerisms came from an article by William Buchanan titled "That Old Mechanics Building and Its Wrestling Matches," which appeared in the *Boston Globe*, February 2, 1964. His quote "one fall to win" came from that same article.

"gingerly on the microphone"—Kaunfer hanging his hat on the microphone is also referenced in "With Harry Kaunfer at Ringside, It Was Always Hello, Hello, Hello," which ran in the *Boston Globe*, April 12, 1981.

"Gravelly delivery"—Kaunfer is described as "gravel-voiced" by William Buchanan in a *Boston Globe* article from April 4, 1982. Kaunfer's habit of drawing out the vowel sounds in certain words and his pronunciation of "New Yuck" are referenced in the *Boston Herald* story titled "A Man with a Voice" by Lawrence Dame. I also listened to an audio recording of Whitey Kaunfer being interviewed by his son.

"Fi-yuv minutes"—Whitey Kaunfer's pronunciation of these words are referenced in Elizabeth Borton's *Boston Herald*, February 18, 1934, article titled "Niagara's Roar vs. Mr. Kaunfer."

"In red tights, The Great Mephisto"—That quote came from "That Old Mechanics Building—And Its Wrestling Matches" by William Buchanan, *Boston Globe*, February 2, 1964.

"beating up his mother"—Mephisto's 1931 arrest for allegedly assaulting his mother was reported in a UP wire story on January 21, 1931, and his later arrests and brushes with the law (of which there were many) were covered by several newspapers. Woronick was arrested on a charge of intoxication for the forty-ninth time according to a February 21, 1961, article in the *Meriden Record*. Other sources included "Champion Wrestler in Meriden Accident," *Hartford Courant*, June 26, 1934; "Wrestler Fined," from the *Chillicothe* (Ohio) *Gazette* on December 19, 1945; "Accused of Beating Mother, Gets Jail," *Meriden Journal*, April 24, 1962; "Psychiatric Test Ordered in Mother Beating Case," *Hartford Courant*, April 25, 1962; "Man Who Beat Mother Is Given Year in Jail," *Hartford Courant*, May 24, 1962.

"Boston Traveler"—Kaunfer drove a truck for the old *Traveler* newspaper for forty years, according to William Buchanan in a *Boston Globe* article from April 4, 1982. Other articles about Kaunfer include his obituary, "Harry Kaunfer, 81 Sports Announcer for 50 Years," from April 7, 1981, in the *Boston Globe*; "Jews in Sports: Meet Whitey—Boston's Mighty Voice" by Ben Bartzoff in the *Wisconsin Jewish Chronicle*, December 6, 1940.

"Pie-puhs, pie-puhs"—This quote came from a *Boston Herald* story by Lawrence Dame titled "A Man with a Voice."

"last tasks of the evening"—*Boston Globe* writer William Buchanan wrote that at the end of the night Kaunfer would telephone the results to all of the major Boston newspapers, which included the *Globe, Herald Traveler, Record-American*, and *Post*. "With Harry Kaunfer at Ringside, It Was Always Hello, Hello, Hello," which ran in the *Boston Globe* on April 12, 1981.

Additional Notes Chapter 1

Information on the wrestlers came from Wrestlingdata.com and Wrestlingclassics .com, 1930 US Census Bureau records, and various books and newspaper articles. Ed Flowers was described as "a nifty colored boy" in a *Cambridge Sentinel* article from April 22, 1933. A story about Mike Tellegen appeared in the Nashua

Telegraph on March 9, 1935. Jackie Nichols turned pro in 1931. Nichols was profiled in the *Bangor Daily News* ("Colorful Jackie Nichols" Bangor Daily News May 28, 1993) and *Discover Maine* magazine ("Jackie Nichols: Maine's Greatest Wrestler," *Discover Maine* magazine, 2012, Volume 9, Issue 2). The Great Mephisto (aka Julius Woronick) was profiled by Oscar Ruhl in an article titled "The Tip-Off," which appeared in the Mansfield (Ohio) *News-Journal*, February 22, 1935. A photo of Mephisto in his tights and showing off his stance appeared with a story titled "Stage Is Set for Flood Relief Mat Show at Amory," by Jack Murray, *Piqua Daily Call*, January 27, 1937. The Jack Pfefer Wrestling Collection at the University of Notre Dame has posters of Mephisto and Dusette.

Descriptions of wrestling moves were drawn from several sources, including the 1912 book *Professional Wrestling* by Ed Wallace Smith; the 1897 book *A Hand-book of Wrestling* by Hugh F. Leonard; the 1934 book *How to Wrestle: Instructions Based on the Work of Frank A. Gotch* by George Robbins of the *Chicago Daily News*; and *From Milo to Londos: The Story of Wrestling Through the Ages* by Nat Fleischer. Another controversial title that provides a glimpse into some aspects of the wrestling business during that time period is the 1937 book *Fall Guys: The Barnums of Bounce* by Marcus Griffin.

Chapter 2: Hometown Boy

The opening quote about Medford rum came from the 1941 film that was based on Stephen Vincent Benét's 1936 short story, "The Devil and Daniel Webster."

I learned about the history of Medford from several sources, including the city of Medford's 2011 Open Space & Recreation Plan Update, *Your House in the Streetcar Suburb: The History and Care of Houses in Medford, Massachusetts*; *Medford in the Victorian Era* by Barbara Kerr; and the city of Medford's website. The city's 1915 to 1930 population figures came from the 1980 Massachusetts Historical Commission Reconnaissance Survey Town Report for Medford.

James D. Murphy was born on June 10, 1885, according to his World War I draft registration card on file with the National Archives and Records Administration in Washington, D.C.

Cicelie was twenty-four years old when she got married, according to the 1911 marriage record from the city of Malden (New England Historic Genealogical Society; Boston, Massachusetts; *Massachusetts Vital Records, 1911–1915*; Volume: 603).

An advertisement in an 1870 business directory for Daniel Lawrence & Sons states that the company had been producing Medford Rum for the past forty-six years, which would put their start date in 1824. A Medford Historical Society plaque in Medford Square confirms this; it states that Daniel Lawrence purchased the John Hall distillery in 1824, and by 1830 it was the only active distillery left in Medford.

The closure of the Lawrence & Sons distillery was reported in the *Boston Globe* on June 18, 1905.

The recipe for Medford Rum Punch appears in the 1888 edition of *The New and Improved Illustrated Bartenders' Manual: Or, How to Mix Drinks of the Present Style* by H. Johnson.

The long history of rum making in Medford is chronicled in several books, including *A Brief History of Medford* by George S. Miller; *Rum: The Epic Story of the Drink That Conquered the World* by Charles A. Coulombe; and *A Bottle of Rum: A History of the New World in Ten Cocktails* by Wayne Curtis. I also gained insight from the Medford Historical Society's website.

The "Ballad of Medford Rum" is mentioned in *The WPA Guide to North Carolina: The Tar Heel State*, a guidebook that was put out by the Federal Writers' Project, a New Deal job program that was part of the Works Progress Administration in the 1930s.

Grantland Rice's creation of the "Four Horsemen" and the age of "myth-making sports journalism" is recounted in the October 17, 1999, *New York Times* article, "The Sports Story That Changed America."

The high school football scene in Massachusetts was detailed in a November 17, 1929, *Boston Globe* article by Louis Lyons titled "It's a Hard Time of Year for the High School Football Hero." Medford's Thanksgiving game against Malden was recounted in the November 29, 1929, *Boston Globe* article titled "Fists Fly as Medford Bows to Malden Before 18,000 Fans" as well as a front-page story that appeared in the *Medford Daily Evening Mercury*.

Murphy's quote "I can score more field goals with my baton than with a football," appeared in the "Live Tips and Topics" sports column in the *Boston Globe* on October 21, 1927.

I found information about Tony Siano in the Fordham University Archives and Special Collections and the Waltham High School 1927 yearbook. Some of his matches against Dropkick Murphy are listed on the www.wrestlingdata.com website.

Chapter 3: Off to College

The description of the Saint Anselm campus came from the 1921–22 edition of the college catalog.

Harry O'Boyle's biographical information came from the National Football League's website; his obituary (Harry O'Boyle, 89, Former Football Player, Lawyer. *Chicago Tribune*. May 9, 1994); the October 1925 edition of the *Notre Dame Alumnus* from the Archives of the University of Notre Dame, and various editions of the University of Notre Dame *Football Review*.

The quote, "the Holy Ghost couldn't have broken into that lineup," appeared in the University of Notre Dame *Football National Championship Review*.

A detailed explanation about the two-platoon system of football came from United Press staff writer Stan Opotowsky's article "Two Platoon System Traced to Rockne's Use of Shock Troops" that appeared in the *Pittsburgh Press* on January 20, 1953.

O'Boyle was described as "one of Rock's fleetest halfbacks" in the 1925 University of Notre Dame *Football Review*.

The reference to uniforms "made of canvas, wool, leather, and felt" came from "The Galloping Ghost: An Interview with Red Grange," *American Heritage* magazine, December 1974.

"one in four medical students"—2022 Osteopathic Medical Profession Report, American Osteopathic Association.

"DOs were holistic before holistic became cool"—This same quote appeared in a November 9, 2018, *U.S. News & World Report* article titled "What's It Mean if My Doctor Is a DO?" by Elaine K. Howley. It also appeared in an August 17, 2018, article by Justin Kaplan titled "The Doctors Without MDs: What Makes Osteopathic Medicine Different?" on WBUR.org.

The Massachusetts College of Osteopathy was originally founded in 1897 as the Boston Institute of Osteopathy, and in 1903 its name was changed to the Massachusetts College of Osteopathy. Murphy attended from 1932–36.

"Dr. Andrew Taylor Still, a physician from Kirksville, Missouri"—His biographical information came from the Museum of Osteopathic Medicine website, and the 1908 *Autobiography of Andrew Taylor Still*.

"Drunkenness is no disgrace but is proof that the man has a disease"—*Osteopathy: Research and Practice* by A. T. Still, page 300.

"Delirium Tremens"—Clinical Osteopathy by Still (A. T.) Research Institute, Chicago. Education Department.

"well fed"—Pages 393–394 of *Practice of Osteopathy: Its Practical Application to the Various Diseases of the Human Body* by Charles Henry Murray, 1912.

Chapter 4: Wrestling Life

Wrestling became an Olympic sport in 708 BC according to the International Olympic Committee website. It was described as "the world's oldest sport" in an article by Gary Mihoces titled, "Ancient Text Proves Wrestling Is Oldest Sport on Record," which appeared in *USA Today* on October 18, 2011. The roots of fake wrestling were recounted in Elizabeth Quill's July 2014 *Smithsonian Magazine* article, "Wrestling Was Fixed, Even in Ancient Rome."

Instances of rigged matches were referenced in the March 11, 1910, *New York Times* article "Tell of Fake Sports."

"In those days, the fairs always had an athletic show"—Colorful Jackie Nichols Joins Maine Sports Hall, *Bangor Daily News*, May 28, 1993.

"attendance record for wrestling"—*Eddie Powers and His House of Magic: A Remembrance of 45 Years at the Boston Garden* by Douglas Crocket, *Boston Globe*, March 18, 1973.

"recovering from a concussion"—*Reading Eagle*, June 30, 1928.

Savoldi was reported to have invented the dropkick in wrestling, according to an article that appeared in the *Lewiston Evening Journal*, August 1, 1933.

The life of Gus Sonnenberg is chronicled on Tim Hornbaker's website, www.legacyofwrestling.com, and the Professional Wrestling Hall of Fame and Museum website.

I interviewed Kaimon Kudo's daughter, Mary Ann Kishiyama, on July 11, 2018.

Descriptions of wrestling injuries are detailed in a piece titled "What Gives in Rasslin'" by C. L. "Steve" McPherson and Oren Arnold that appeared in *Collier's Weekly on* October 29, 1949.

"It isn't sport; it is show business,"—Quote from an article titled "Jake's Juggernauts" by Jack Miley in *Collier's Weekly*, October 22, 1938, pp. 56–77. Note: Pfefer's name is occasionally spelled Pfeffer.

"10 Wrestlers Reportedly Died on the Mat in 1936"—*Life*, January 25, 1937.

"gimmicks in the ring"—"Wrestlers Wear Strange Costumes for a New Gag," *Life*, April 29, 1940.

Wrestlers getting "pelted by paper clips" came from an article titled "My Father the Thing" by Joe Jares, *Sports Illustrated*, March 21, 1966.

"Dean Detton"—*Life*, January 25, 1937.

Count Von Zuppe is featured in the article "German Aristocrat Not So Gentlemanly in the Ring," *Reading Eagle*, September 12, 1936. His "satin robe embroidered with an iron cross" is described in *The American Legion*, Volume 40, No. 10, October 1946.

Zimba Parker was called an "Ethiopian savage," in the December 3, 1935, edition of the *North Adams Transcript*, and was dubbed the "Brown Bomber" in the *Reading Eagle* on September 11, 1936.

"take an oath"—"A Gorgeous Era in Wrestling," *Los Angeles Times*, December 14, 1997.

The quote "Freaks I Love and They're My Specialty," came from the article "Jake's Juggernauts" by Jack Miley in *Collier's Weekly*, October 22, 1938.

"sometimes with a hyphen (drop-kick)"—an instructional illustration appears in the *Lewiston Evening Journal*, October 24, 1925.

The evolution of footballs becoming longer and slimmer is detailed in "How Did the Pigskin Get Its Shape?" by Jimmy Stamp, *Smithsonian Magazine*, October 5, 2012.

"Doug Flutie pulled it off on New Year's Day"—Flutie converts first dropkick since 1941 championship, ESPN.com, January 2, 2006.

"The last successful dropkick prior to Flutie's was in 1941"—"Patriots Lose in Finale, but Playoffs on the Their Mind," *Boston Globe*, January 2, 2006.

"dropkick"—*Historical Dictionary of Wrestling* by John Grasso.

Abe Coleman was known for his two-footed kick that he copied from kangaroos according to his obituary that appeared in the *New York Times* on April 2, 2007. Coleman introducing the kangaroo kick to wrestling was also mentioned in an October 20, 1932, article in *Baltimore Evening Sun*.

Savoldi's dropkick style can be seen on film in "All-In Wrestling" a British Pathé newsreel from 1934 that shows a match in Los Angeles between Savoldi and Man Mountain Dean.

Chapter 5: The Politics of Grappling

According to Tim Honbaker's book *National Wrestling Alliance: The Untold Story of the Monopoly That Strangled Professional Wrestling*, "professional wrestling's popularity reached a peak during the Great Depression" and the "Strangler" Lewis match against Jim Londos at Wrigley Field in Chicago in 1934 broke attendance records.

The reference to "drawing bigger box-office returns" came from a November 15, 1931, *Boston Globe* article by Joe Williams titled "Why the Great Popularity of the Once-Despised Sport of Wrestling?"

An article by Milton MacKaye in the *Saturday Evening Post* from December 14, 1935, stated that wrestling was grossing $5 million a year and was "the most solvent of sports."

Efforts to regulate wrestling were often tied to the sport of boxing. Many incarnations of wrestling legislation can be traced back to James J. Frawley, a big, athletic man who served in the New York State Senate from 1903 to 1914. A former boxer himself, Frawley worked in construction and was connected to Tammany Hall, and he spent years lobbying to legalize boxing. As early as 1903 he introduced a bill to legalize boxing. Under his plan, a state athletic commission would oversee the sport, all boxers and promoters would have to be licensed, and the state would get to collect 5 percent of gross receipts from matches. Any fighter who was found to be taking part in fake or sham matches would be suspended for six months and disqualified upon the second offense. It took a while, but when his legislation eventually passed in 1911, it became known as the "Frawley Law." The statute served as a model for other states to follow. In the years to come, whenever lawmakers decided to regulate wrestling, they often turned to the same template. Frawley went down in history as the father of the state boxing law, but in retrospect, he was the forefather of wrestling legislation as well.

"April 1930"—"Wrestling Placed Under New Status," *New York Times*, April 9, 1930.

"May 19, 1930"—Chapter 43 Resolve providing for an investigation by a special COMMISSION relative TO PROFESSIONAL BOXING AND WRESTLING. Acts and Resolves Passed by the General Court of Massachusetts in the Year 1930.

The hearings in Lawrence and Lowell were covered in the *Lowell Sun* on October 17, 1930.

"asked for more time"—House Bill No. 290, December 31, 1930. Report of the Special Commission Appointed to Study Professional Boxing and Wrestling.

1931 House Bill 1375. Report of the Special Commission Relative to Professional Boxing and Wrestling, February 1931.

I drew from many *Boston Globe* articles about legislative hearings and proposals to regulate wrestling, including "To Start Wrestling and Boxing Inquiry," May 20, 1930; "Boxing Wrestling Go Under Probe: First Hearing Today at State House," October 14, 1930; "Hot Wrestling Debate at Hearing," February 18, 1932; 'Asserts 99 Percent of Bouts on Level," February 9, 1933; "Langone Decides He Won't Quit Senate," April 25, 1933; "Senate Rejects Langone's Bill," April 26, 1933; "Calls Wrestling, Hockey 'Rackets': Bills Introduced for Their Supervision," February 13, 1936.

Casson's "dull spectacle" quote appeared in the *Boston Globe*, March 12, 1931.

I obtained information about legislators from the "Public Officials of Massachusetts" directories for the years 1929 through 1934.

The Regulation of Boxing: A History and Comparative Analysis of Policies Among American States, Robert G. Rodriguez, McFarland & Company Inc. Publishers, 2008.

Additional Notes Chapter 5

One early move to regulate pro wrestling took place in May 1921, when the governor of New York signed a bill that put boxing and wrestling under the supervision of a state athletic commission. The newly created commission would be made up of three unpaid members who would establish common rules for wrestling matches. The new law stated that the commissioners would "prescribe the length or duration of such contest, the manner in which the contestants shall engage in such contest and such further safeguards and conditions as shall insure [sic] fair, sportsmanlike and scientific wrestling contests."

Similar legislation passed in Nebraska in 1921 and proved to be profitable for the state. It put wrestling under the supervision of a state commission, and required wrestlers, boxers, officials, and managers to be licensed. The state sent inspectors to watch matches and 5 percent of admissions receipts went to the state. When it went into effect in July 1921, it also included a "color line" measure, prohibiting that black and white athletes could not compete against each other in boxing or wrestling.

In 1926 Louisiana considered a measure to regulate wrestling. It required wrestlers to pay a $25 license fee and any wrestler who was found to have faked a contest would be suspended from competing in any bouts for six months. Bills related to wrestling were considered in Oklahoma (1927), California (had a commission by 1925), West Virginia, Colorado, and Ohio (1933); in 1933, Oklahoma and Illinois considered banning wrestling entirely (Illinois ultimately did).

Information on Abraham Casson came from several sources, including the following *Boston Globe* articles: "Judge Casson of Municipal Court Dies," June 21, 1961; "Casson Appointed to City Legal Post," December 4, 1931; "Garden Buys 60% of Bruins," October 12, 1951.

Boston Bruins founder Charles Francis Adams was the chairman and principal owner of the First National Stores supermarket chain, and Casson represented him at legislative hearing on March 14, 1934, according to a *Boston Globe* article titled "Some Farms 'Sweat Shops': O'Brien Blames Dealers for Low Milk Price."

The quotes from Henry Cauthen appeared in a column by Carter "Scoop" Latimer in the *Greenville News* (South Carolina), February 3, 1934.

"tights and flesh"—*Boston Traveler*, February 2, 1953.

"female jackasses"—*Berkshire Evening Eagle*, February 6, 1953, page 15.

"letter to the editor"—*Springfield Union*, February 10, 1953, page 28.

Legislation filed in Massachusetts included 1950 House Bill 0567: An Act Relating to Non-Participation by Women in Wrestling and Roller Derbies; 1951 House Bill 0465: An Act Prohibiting Women from Participating in the Sport of Wrestling; 1953 House Bill 1628. An Act Prohibiting Women from Participating in The Sport of Wrestling; 1954 House Bill 2188. An Act Prohibiting Women from Participating in The Sport of Wrestling; and 1963 Senate Bill 0491. An Act Prohibiting Wrestling Between Women and Midgets, archived in the State Library of Massachusetts.

The instance where someone "smashed the neck off of a glass Coca-Cola bottle" was reported in the *Evening Independent* (St. Petersburg, Florida) on March 14, 1935.

On January 26, 1934, the Associated Press reported that the New York State Athletic Commission had rewritten the regulations governing wrestling.

"immediately disqualified him"—*Lowell Sun*, January 8, 1935.

Chapter 6: On the Road

Murphy's Thanksgiving Day match was reported in the Lewiston *Daily Sun* on November 29, 1934. Results of his match at North Street Arena in Salem the following day appeared in the *Boston Globe* on December 1, 1934. The reference to Murphy even wrestling on Christmas was recounted in the Lewiston *Evening Journal* on December 26, 1934.

Dropkick Murphy was called a "Southern playboy" in the January 4, 1935, edition of the Lewiston *Daily Sun*.

Thomas Anthony "Tony" Siano was originally from Waltham, and played center and was an All-American at Fordham. Siano went on to play two seasons in the NFL.

Source of information on NFL salaries: *From Sandlots to the Super Bowl: The National Football League, 1920–1967* by Craig R. Coenen, University of Tennessee Press, 2005.

An article titled "Evolution of the NFL Player" on the NFL Football Operations website chronicles the history of pro football and how it's changed over the years.

The average playing career of an NFL player back then only lasted two years, according to *The Business of Professional Sports* by Paul D. Staudohar, ed. J. A. Mangan, University of Illinois Press, 1991.

St. Nicholas Palace (aka Royal Windsor Palace, or the "Bucket of Blood") is referenced in the *Reading Eagle* on October 21, 1943, and *New York Post* on September 11, 1935.

The account of Murphy breaking his teeth came from a January 15, 1937, *New York Times* article, "Levin Tosses Murphy in Hippodrome Match."

News of Gus Sonnenberg's crash was reported in the *Nashua Telegraph* on July 19, 1932.

The *Boston Globe* covered Sonnenberg's trial in detail in a series of articles, including "Sonnenberg Taken for Auto Fatality," July 30, 1932; "90 Days In Jail to Sonnenberg: Wrestler Appeals Term and Fine of $100," August 3, 1932; "Sonnenberg's Feet Unsteady: Bartender So Testifies at Lawrence Trial," February 28, 1933; "Sonnenberg Tells Own Story Today: Wrestler's Witnesses Deny He Drank," March 1, 1933; "Sonnenberg on Witness Stand: Denies He Drank," March 2, 1933; "Gus Sonnenberg Cleared by Jury," *Boston Globe*, March 3, 1933.

The hit-and-run charge against Paul Bowser's wife Cora was reported in the *Boston Globe* on March 12, 1936, and the *Newton Graphic* newspaper on March 13, 1936. Cora Livingston was profiled in a feature story by E. I. Leeds Jr. titled "Woman Won as Wrestler" that appeared in the *Brooklyn Daily Eagle* on September 23, 1928.

The 1950–51 season marked the first appearance of black players in the NBA. The NFL effectively banned African Americans from 1933 to 1945.

Jack Claybourne and Jim "The Black Panther" Mitchell are featured in the University of Kentucky Libraries Notable Kentucky African Americans Database. I also read the John Cosper's article "'The Black Panther' Jim Mitchell" on the Eat Sleep Wrestle website and viewed the Jim Mitchell collection on the website of the Frazier History Museum (an affiliate of the Smithsonian Institution) in Kentucky, and read "Black Like Me," on the Wrestling Perspective website. I also watched *Black Sam's Statue*, a film by Elliott Marquis.

The stories I referenced in *The Afro-American* appeared in the January 8, 1944, edition of the paper.

Jesse James was the stage name for Demitros Stephanos Tzitzikas. The drama leading up to the championship was reported in the Danville *Morning News* on April 25, 1938, and in several other articles, including "McCloskey to Award Mat Winner Championship Belt," *Harrisburg Telegraph*, April 22, 1938. The anti-climactic result of the championship was recounted in the story "Curfew Causes End of Bout in Hour, 43 Mins," from the *Evening News* on April 27, 1938.

Reading, Pennsylvania, was called the pretzel capital of the world in the April 1948 issue of the *Historical Review of Berks County*.

The quote "the crowd wants blood" came from a profile of Bert Bertolini that appeared in the *Reading Eagle* on February 16, 1937.

LaBelle's nickname "the French mat wizard" appeared in the article "Murphy to Quit Wrestling If He Loses to LaBelle" in the *Reading Eagle* on February 25, 1940. A photo of him (and his bald head) appeared in the *Reading Eagle* on March 15, 1940. The result of the bout being declared a draw was reported in the *Reading Eagle* on February 28, 1940.

Census records show that in 1940 Murphy and his wife Marie were living at 25 St. Mary Street with Murphy's mother, and their baby boy, Richard. Murphy's parents owned the house, which was a single-family dwelling and worth about $6,000 at the time. Their neighbors on St. Mary Street were mainly working-class professionals with modest incomes: a stenographer who made $1,040 a year; an attorney who earned $1,560; a trolley repairman made $2,020; the sales-man made $1,800; an engineer on his street made $2,057. Meanwhile, Murphy was making $5,000 a year as a professional wrestler. Murphy may not have known it at the time, but he was the wealthiest guy on the block. And he had big plans.

Additional Notes Chapter 6

Dropkick Murphy's second child, David, was born on May 8, 1940.

The reference to the part-time police officer directing traffic in Acton came from the Board of Selectmen's Report from the Town of Acton Annual Report for the year ending December 31, 1940.

I found information on Ebenezer Davis in the 1890 book *Acton in History* by J. W. Lewis.

Houck's quotes came from an article in the Acton *Assabet Valley Beacon* news-paper on May 18, 1967, "Juvenile Delinquency Problem Growing in Acton; Rate Is Up."

As of March 1921, there were no state-run hospitals for inebriates in the United States, the last having closed in 1920, according to a *New York Times* article "No Inebriate Hospitals," on March 21, 1921.

Dr. Sheldon's Sanitarium in Springboro, Pennsylvania, promised alcoholics and addicts that they could be cured completely: "we have no failures."

The lack of treatment options for alcoholics was illustrated in a notable survey that was conducted by E. H. L. Corwin and Elizabeth V. Cunningham. They found that in 1940 there were still no state institutions specializing in treating alcoholics exclusively. Only twenty-two private institutions focused on treating addiction and about a dozen private psychiatric institutions that admitted alcoholic patients on a regular basis.

"dresser drawer over a photographer's"—*Now Pitching, Bob Feller* by Bob Feller and Bill Gilbert.

"Meet me on the hotel mezzanine"—*The Cleveland Indians* by Franklin A. Lewis.

"\he got involved with A.A."—*The Cooperstown Chronicles: Baseball's Colorful Characters, Unusual Lives and Strange Demises* by Frank Russo.

"men to be committed for up to two years"—*The Journal of Inebriety*, Volume 18, page 37.

"The Keeley "Gold Cure" for Inebriety," *British Medical Journal*, July 9, 1892; "Author of Keeley Cure Dead," *New York Times*, February 22, 1900; "If Dr. Keeley Could See You Now, You'd Be Headed for 'Jabs,'" *Wall Street Journal* article by Cynthia Crossen, December 31, 2007.

The number of Keeley Institutes is referenced in Suzanne S. Brent's December 1996 dissertation, "The History of Alcoholism Treatment in the United States and Slaying the Dragon: The History of Addiction Treatment and Recovery in America" by William L. White. The number of Keeley Branch Institutes declined from 118 in 1893 to 35 in 1916. Only four were left in 1935.

"There were even auxiliary groups for members' wives, mothers, sisters and daughters"—George A. Barclay, *Journal of the Illinois State Historical Society* (1908–1984) Volume 57, No. 4 (Winter 1964), pp. 341–365.

The mayor of Woburn's proposal to build a cage was covered in a series of articles in the *Boston Globe*.

I learned about the Neal Institute from an article titled "The Neal Cure Ends Drink Habit in Three Days," that was published on August 7, 1910, in the *Boston Globe*. Another helpful source was a book published in 1915 by James E. Bruce, the treasurer and general manager of the Neal Institute Company, titled *The Drinker Defended and Fortified*.

"How Did I Learn?"—*Tallahassee Democrat*, Sunday, April 16, 1939, page 7.

"Hemsley 'Through Drinking Forever,'" *Minneapolis Star*, April 18, 1940.

"the number of A.A. groups continued to grow"—*A Biography of Mrs. Marty Mann: The First Lady of Alcoholics Anonymous*, by Sally Brown, David R. Brown

"Problem with Alcohol?" Advertisement for A.A. meetings at Bellows Farm, *Assabet Valley Beacon*, January 18, 1968.

"Alcoholics Anonymous," Acton *Beacon*, June 26, 1945.

Chapter 7: Health Farmer
William Muldoon's quote came from the article, "Making Men Over" by Isaac F. Marcosson in the October 1912 edition of *Munsey's Magazine*.

Bill Brown's quote came from a profile titled "Farm and Ringside" by Earl Sparling in the May 18, 1935, edition of the *New Yorker*.

Wamesit Health Farm was described in Joyce Tsai's March 5, 2011, Lowell *Sun* article, "Tewksbury Farm Founder Pulled No Punches." An account of Jack Sharkey training at Flaherty's health farm was reported in the *Boston Globe* on June 17, 1924. Several stories about Honeyboy Finnegan training at the farm appeared in the *Globe* in the 1920s.

I found a lengthy profile of William Muldoon in "Spartacus in Westchester," which appeared in the *New Yorker* on July 16, 1927.

"Olympia, a hygienic institute"—"The Life Story of William Muldoon," as told to his friend Ed. Van Every, *Ottawa Citizen*, February 6, 1929.

"I don't take alcoholics"—The Ogden (Utah) *Standard-Examiner*, December 27, 1920.

"I have no faith in alcohol"—*Manchester* (Vermont) *Journal*, January 6, 1916.

"refused to let him smoke"—Bare Knuckle Boxing Hall of Fame website.

"more energy than a ton of benzedrine inhalers"—*The Wrestling Scene* by Guy LeBow, New York, Homecrafts Sports Division, 1950.

I found an advertisement for Bowler Farms in the June 22, 1916, edition of the *Boston Medical and Surgical Journal*, Volume 174, Issue 2.

Bowler's techniques were detailed in "Old Dartmouth Men Find Youth on Health Farm," a July 25, 1920, feature story in the *Boston Sunday Post*.

William Muldoon's health farm in White Plains, New York, was the focus of the article "At the Maples," that was published in the *Washington Times* on July 23, 1895.

Information about Valleyhead Hospital in Carlisle came from the 1941 book *Old Houses and Families of Carlisle, Mass.*, and a February 6, 2004, *Carlisle Mosquito* article by Ellen Millier titled "Valleyhead: 50 Years of Healing on South Street."

Other sources included: "Sylvia Plath"—Sylvia Plath's autograph journal, 1950–1953, Smith College Libraries, and "Jacqueline Kennedy"—"Jackie Oh!" by Kitty Kelley, 1978. *Jacqueline Kennedy Onassis: A Life Beyond Her Wildest Dreams* by Darwin Porter and Danforth Prince, 2014.

"I underwent a rather brief"—*The Letters of Sylvia Plath*, pp. 655–656.

Chapter 8: War Time

"Bowser's Matmen Again Aid Soldiers; Part of Receipts Tonight to Go for Sports Gear," *Boston Globe*, May 13, 1942.

A story about Sonnenberg enlisting in the Navy appeared in the *New Castle* (Pennsylvania) *News* on October 16, 1942. A photo of Sonnenberg teaching wrestling at the United States Naval Training Center Bainbridge appeared in the Frederick Post on July 23, 1943.

Winn Robbins spoke about his experience as a firefighter responding to the Cocoanut Grove fire in an interview posted on the Boston Fire Historical Society's website.

I also got information about the Cocoanut Grove fire from the city of Boston's November 28, 1942, "Report Concerning the Cocoanut Grove Fire," by Boston Fire Commissioner William Arthur Reilly.

An account of the celebrations in Acton at the end of World War II "V-J Day Comes to Acton," Acton *Beacon*, August 17, 1945.

Chapter 9: Life and Detox

The references to "one fellow was very fond of playing the ponies" and the quotes "Don't let him touch me!" and "the best worker I've got on the place" came from Dink Carroll's June 11, 1943, "Playing the Field" column in the *Montreal Gazette*.

David F. Egan, a renowned Boston sportswriter who wrote provocative columns under the pseudonym, "The Colonel."

On October 23, 1948, *Pittsburgh Courier* reported that Egan smuggling in bottles of liquor to Dropkick Murphy's is mentioned in David Halberstam's book, *Summer of '49* and Leigh Montville's book *Ted Williams: The Biography of an American Hero*. Ben Bradlee's book *The Kid: The Immortal Life of Ted Williams* also contains important details about Egan's life, including an amusing tidbit from a *Boston Traveler* reporter who recalled how Ted Williams once said, "if someone came in that door and said, 'Dave Egan just dropped dead,' I'd say, 'Good.'"

Information on the Brink's Robbery and Joseph Sylvester Banfield came from the FBI's website and articles in the *Boston Globe*.

The story of Jackie Gleason coming to Bellows Farm was recounted by several people I interviewed, but Dropkick Murphy's son David gave me the most detailed recollection of the event. He also told me how the picture of Jackie Gleason became a fixture at the farm.

Gleason's friendship with Rocky Marciano and his efforts to get into shape by training with him are referenced in William A. Henry's book, *The Great One: The Life and Legend of Jackie Gleason* and Mike Stanton's book *Unbeaten: Rocky Marciano's Fight for Perfection in a Crooked World*. Stanton's book also mentions that Marciano talked about opening a health club with Gleason and Toots Shor, the owner of a popular Manhattan restaurant and saloon.

Joseph ("Jumping Joe") Savoldi Jr.'s participation in the McGregor Mission is detailed in an article titled "OSS in Action: The Mediterranean and European Theaters" on the U.S. National Park Service website.

Savoldi's withdrawal from Notre Dame for disciplinary reasons stemming from his divorce proceedings was reported in the *New York Times* under the headline "Notre Dame Eleven Loses Joe Savoldi" on November 18, 1930.

The Regan brothers hailed from County Mayo, Ireland—Shaun, Tim, and Patrick, according to Patrick Regan's obituary in the *Sentinel & Enterprise*. The quote "Everybody here seems Irish," is from an April 5, 1949, story in the Lowell *Sun*.

References to Clyde Steeves, Buddy Hayes, Charlie Fusari, and Rocky Graziano training at Bellows Farm appeared in Frank Sargent's sports column in the Lowell *Sun*, June 16, 1949.

"It's the air in Acton," he said—*Young at Heart: The Story of Johnny Kelley, Boston's Marathon Man* by Frederick Lewis, Richard A. Johnson.

The *Boston Globe* reported on Joe Rindone training at Bellows Farm on July 19, 1951.

Chapter 10: The Fighters

Biographical information about Jimmy Carter can be found on the International Boxing Hall of Fame's website.

Valenti's quote about Dropkick having a "better gym" appeared in the *Boston Evening American* on March 30, 1953.

Carter's quote that he would "never make predictions" came from an April 24, 1953, Associated Press article.

On April 25, 1953, the front page of the *Boston Globe* declared "Collins Floored 9 Times as Carter Wins," but according to most other reports, Collins went down ten times. The *New York Times* and *Time* magazine reported Collins was floored ten times. On April 26, 1953, *Globe* writer Jerry Nason acknowledged this discrepancy when he wrote that Collins was "knocked down nine times (some say ten) and unleashed the outraged cries of a national TV audience."

Robert K. Christenberry's quotes about the fight appeared in the *New York Times* on April 25, 1953, under the headline "Brutal Title Fight Shocks TV Viewers." The *Boston Globe* also published Christenberry's comments.

Jimmy Carter said the fight "turned my stomach" in the May 7, 1953, edition of *Jet* magazine.

Reaction to the fight came from the April 26, 1953, edition of the Bridgeport, Connecticut, *Sunday Herald*; "Bout Called Deplorable," *New York Times*, April 26, 1953.

I interviewed Tony DeMarco on September 17, 2014.

I found a biography of George Araujo on the Rhode Island College James P. Adams Library Digital Commons website.

The quote "just like we practiced at Dropkick's" appeared in the *Boston Daily Record* on July 14, 1954.

DeMarco's quote "Wiseguys were part of boxing" came from an April 1, 2008, ESPN article by Don Stradley titled, "DeMarco Hoodwink Made Saxton the April Fool."

Chapter 11: Ghosts of Bellows Farm

Many quotes from Dropkick Murphy throughout the book came from a lengthy article by Joe Purcell, "Dropkick Murphy Shuts Up Shop" from the *Boston Sunday Herald Traveler*, December 19, 1971.

The quote "Help, fire, fire!" appeared in the *Boston Evening American* on November 5, 1957. Other accounts of the fire at Bellows Farm appeared in "Acton's Worst Fire Claims 2 Lives," in the Acton *Beacon* on November 7, 1957, and "State Opens Probe of Blaze in Acton Which Took 2 Lives," from the *Boston Globe* on November 6, 1957.

Reinert Anderson had been born in Norway on September 17, 1889, according to his World War II draft card that's on file at the National Archives in St. Louis, Missouri.

SOURCES

Beekman, Scott. *Ringside: A History of Professional Wrestling in America*. Westport, CT: Praeger Publishers, 2006.

Bradlee, Ben. *The Kid: The Immortal Life of Ted Williams*. Back Bay Books/Little, Brown, and Company, 2014.

Brady, Edward T. *Last In My Class: How Humor Helped Me Survive Alcoholism*. Bloomington, IN: Xlibris Corp. 2001.

Brown, Jeremy. *Influenza: The Quest to Cure the Deadliest Disease in History*. New York City: Touchstone, 2018.

Camp, Walter. *Walter Camp's Book of College Sports*. New York: Century Company, 1893.

Capouya, John. *Gorgeous George*. New York City: HarperCollins Publishers, 2008.

Cosper, John. *The Original Black Panther: The Life & Legacy of Jim Mitchell*. Independently published, 2019.

Coulombe, Charles A. *Rum: The Epic Story of the Drink That Conquered the World*. New York City: Kensington Publishing Corporation, 2005.

DeMarco, Tony, and Ellen Zappala. *Nardo: Memoirs of a Boxing Champion*. Mineola, NY: Legas Publishing, 2011.

Fleischer, Nat. *From Milo to Londos: The Story of Wrestling Through the Ages*. New York: Ring, 1936.

Flood, Joe. *The Fires: How a Computer Formula, Big Ideas, and the Best of Intentions Burned Down New York City—and Determined the Future of Cities*. New York City: Penguin Publishing Group, 2010.

Ford, Erwin H. *George V. Higgins: The Life and Writings*. Jefferson, NC: McFarland & Company, Inc. Publishers, 2014.

Halberstam, David. *Summer of '49*. New York City: HarperCollins, 1990.

Henry, William A. *The Great One: The Life and Legend of Jackie Gleason*. New York: Doubleday, 1992.

Higgins, George V. *Cogan's Trade: A Thriller*. New York City: Knopf Doubleday Publishing Group, 2011.

Hornbaker, Tim. *Legends of Pro Wrestling: 150 Years of Headlocks, Body Slams, and Piledrivers*. New York City: Skyhorse Publishing, 2012.

Kerr, Barbara. *Glimpses of Medford: Selections from the Historical Register*. Charleston, SC: The History Press, 2007.

Lentz, Harris M. *Biographical Dictionary of Professional Wrestling*. Jefferson, NC: McFarland & Company, Inc. Publishers, 2003.

Lewis, Frederick, and Richard A. Johnson. *Young at Heart: The Story of Johnny Kelley, Boston's Marathon Man*. Cambridge, MA: Rounder Books, 2005.

Maloney, Ralph. *The 24-Hour Drink Book: A Guide to Executive Survival*. New York City: Ivan Obolensky Inc., 1962.

Marrin, Albert. *Very, Very, Very Dreadful: The Influenza Pandemic of 1918*. Knopf Books for Young Readers, 2018.

Montville, Leigh. *Ted Williams: The Biography of an American Hero*. New York City: Doubleday, 2004.

Morris, Dee. *Medford: A Brief History*. Charleston, SC: The History Press, 2009.

O'Keefe, Joseph James and Bob, Considine. *The Crime that Nearly Paid: The Inside Story of One of the Most Famous Hold-ups in the History of Crime*. London: Andre Deutsch, Ltd., 1962.

Oliver, Greg, and Steven Johnson. *The Pro Wrestling Hall of Fame: The Heels*. Toronto: ECW Press, 2007.

Pointer, Ray. *The Art and Inventions of Max Fleischer: American Animation Pioneer*. Jefferson, NC: McFarland & Company, Inc. Publishers, 2017.

Riess, Steven A. *Sports in America from Colonial Times to the Twenty-First Century: An Encyclopedia*. London and New York: Taylor & Francis, 2015.

Russo, Frank. *The Cooperstown Chronicles: Baseball's Colorful Characters, Unusual Lives, and Strange Demises*. Lanham, MD: Rowman & Littlefield Publishers, 2014.

Sammarco, Anthony Mitchell. *Images of America: Medford*. Charleston, SC: Arcadia Publishing, 1999.

Sandow, Billy., Lewis, Ed. *The Sandow-Lewis Library: Presenting the Sandow-Lewis Kinetic Stress System of Physical Training*. United States: Sandow-Lewis, Inc., 1926.

Saunders, Patricia. *Medford, Then & Now*. Charleston, SC: Arcadia Publishing, 2005.

Schmidt, Raymond. *Shaping College Football: The Transformation of an American Sport, 1919–1930*. Syracuse, NY: Syracuse University Press, 2007.

Schuster, David G. *Neurasthenic Nation: America's Search for Health, Happiness, and Comfort, 1869–1920*. Ithaca, NY: Rutgers University Press, 2011.

Shabazz, Julian L. D. *Black Stars of Professional Wrestling*. United States: Awesome Records, 1999.

Stanton, Mike. *Unbeaten: Rocky Marciano's Fight for Perfection in a Crooked World*. New York City: Henry Holt and Company, 2018.

Thesz, Lou and Bauman, Kit. *Hooker*. Gallatin, TN: Crowbar Press, 2011.

Tracy, Sarah W. *Alcoholism in America: From Reconstruction to Prohibition*. Baltimore: The Johns Hopkins University Press, 2005.

Trowbridge, Carol. *Andrew Taylor Still, 1828–1917*. Kirksville, MO: Truman State University Press, 1991.

White, William L. *Slaying the Dragon: The History of Addiction Treatment and Recovery in America*. Normal, IL: Chestnut Health Systems, 1998.

Periodicals

Aghajanian, Liana. "The Legend of Ali Baba: The Incredible Story of Armenian Genocide Survivor & World Wrestling Champ Harry Ekizian." *Ianyan* magazine, April 21, 2014.

Appel, Jacob M. "Physicians Are Not Bootleggers: The Short, Peculiar Life of the Medicinal Alcohol Movement." *Bulletin of the History of Medicine,* Johns Hopkins University Press, Volume 82, No. 2, Summer 2008.

Corwin, E. H. L., and Elizabeth V. Cunningham. "Institutional Facilities for the Treatment of Alcoholism," *Quarterly Journal of Studies on Alcohol*, 1944.

Maguire, Brendan, and John F. Wozniak. "Racial and Ethnic Stereotypes in Professional Wrestling." *Social Science Journal* 24, no. 3 (1987).

Oliver, Greg. "Cowboy Hughes: The Maritime Legacy of Len Hughes," *SLAM! Wrestling*, January 18, 2009.

Quill, Elizabeth. "Wrestling Was Fixed, Even in Ancient Rome." *Smithsonian Magazine*, July 2014.

Rupp, Rebecca. "Rum: The Spirit That Fueled a Revolution," *National Geographic*, April 10, 2015.

Schuster, David G. "Neurasthenia and a Modernizing America," *JAMA*. November 5, 2003. https://jamanetwork.com/journals/jama/fullarticle/197572

"Seeing Fans: Representations of Fandom in Media and Popular Culture," *Bloomsbury Publishing USA*, pages 33–43.

Stone, Gregory P. "Wrestling: The Great American Passion Play," *Sport: Approaches to the Study of Sport*, Volume 1, pages 185–215.

Tracy, Sarah Whitney. "The Foxborough Experiment: Medicalizing Inebriety at the Massachusetts Hospital for Dipsomaniacs and Inebriates," Ph.D. Dissertation, 1992.

White, April. "Inside a Nineteenth-Century Quest to End Addiction," *JSTOR Daily*, December 14, 2016.

Zashin, Stephen S. "Bodyslam from the Top Rope: Unequal Bargaining Power and Professional Wrestling's Failure to Unionize," *University of Miami Entertainment & Sports Law Review*, 1995.

ABOUT THE AUTHOR

Emily Sweeney is a staff reporter at the *Boston Globe* and author of the books *Boston Organized Crime* and *Gangland Boston*. A proud native of Dorchester, she also appears in *Bloody Boston*, a two-part documentary special on the Reelz channel; *Stranger Than Fiction: The True Story of Whitey Bulger, Southie, and The Departed*, a bonus feature on the DVD of the Oscar-winning movie *The Departed*; and the forthcoming Netflix series *How to Become a Mob Boss*.

Dropkick Murphy is set in 10-point Sabon, which was designed by the German-born typographer and designer Jan Tschichold (1902–1974) in the period 1964–1967. It was released jointly by the Linotype, Monotype, and Stempel type foundries in 1967. Copyeditor for this project was Shannon LeMay-Finn. The book was designed by Brad Norr Design, Minneapolis, Minnesota, and typeset by New Best-set Typesetters Ltd.

CPSIA information can be obtained
at www.ICGtesting.com
Printed in the USA
JSHW020040150523
41518JS00004B/4